YOUR GIFTED CHILD

YOUR
GIFTED CHILD

A Guide for Parents

by

FLORENCE N. BRUMBAUGH

and

BERNARD ROSHCO

HENRY HOLT AND COMPANY   NEW YORK

Contents

INTRODUCTION

Why Parents Must Help the Gifted

MOST CHILDREN have more natural ability than is ever realized. Much of this capability remains forever undiscovered, unawakened, and unused.

Undoubtedly, if more children were given the opportunities and encouragement to demonstrate what gifts they have, and to develop those they reveal, the proportion of youngsters rated as gifted would increase. This book is intended to help parents help their children uncover and develop their inborn abilities.

In recent years many American families have returned to the pioneer tradition of "do-it-yourself." Shortages of skilled outside help have forced many to acquire their own skills in order to meet their material needs.

Another sphere of American life that can best be improved by families doing a large part of the improving themselves is education. The education of their children is a responsibility that many parents have been neglecting. Although a large part of this job belongs to the schools, the basic responsibility for developing a child's giftedness still rests with his parents.

With the current shortage of school facilities and teachers, with the constantly expanding school population, with the vast variety of courses and services that the public schools attempt to provide, the task of offering a basic education for all children is more than many schools can handle. Comparatively few schools have been able to take on the added burden of giving gifted children the kind of education they need.

The identification and education of gifted children is therefore a do-it-yourself project that has to be a joint undertaking of parents and child. The school helps, of course, and plays an indispensable role in educating the gifted, but very often the difference between the full growth of a gifted child's abilities and only mediocre achievement depends on the role that parents play in their child's development.

In recent years enough has been learned about the gifted to correct many of the mistaken ideas of past years. The impressions and training gifted children receive from their parents before starting school, and during the early school years, are now known to be especially important.

As Paul Witty, psychologist and educator who has been a distinguished pioneer in pleading the cause of the gifted child, has written: "A major part of the educator's responsibility will be to work with parents in the development of a clearer understanding of the gifted child and his needs."

This book is intended to serve as a guide for parents who want a better understanding of gifted children and the special assistance they need in order to have the best chance to develop their gifts. The suggested methods and activities are based on the research of many psychologists and educators and on seventeen years of experience in educating gifted children gained by one of the co-authors. She has been the principal of the Hunter College Elementary School ever since it was established as a school for intellectually gifted children. This unique institution is a laboratory school supported by the New York City Board of Higher Education for the study and education of gifted children and for teacher training.

This book is a guide rather than a blueprint. It offers principles and makes suggestions that will enable parents to work out their own ways of handling specific situations. Since every child is an individual, each must be handled differently. But since all children have certain qualities in common, there are principles and techniques that can be applied to all of them.

Whether or not a child is "gifted" in the sense that educators and psychologists use the term, he has some special abilities. All children should be assisted in developing such gifts. The following pages explain what can be done to encourage the further development of every child who has superior abilities.

Part I

UNDERSTANDING GIFTEDNESS

CHAPTER ONE

What Gifted Children Are Like

GIFTED CHILDREN have become like the weather. Everybody is talking about them. Unlike the weather—and unlike the past—almost everybody is talking about them favorably. As one educator noted, "The gifted were once almost completely neglected. Now everybody is hugging them to death."

In Washington, government officials proclaim that more scientifically trained persons are needed to save the nation. The gifted, they say, must fill the gap. Around the country an increasing number of educators announce they are intensifying their teaching programs in order to enable the gifted to acquire more knowledge in less time. Parents read newspapers in which the new attitude toward the gifted is reported. They watch television programs on which a number of gifted children have performed as quiz contestants. As a result, they wonder if their own children might be fortunate enough to be gifted.

Giftedness is becoming fashionable. One bright teen-age girl commented, "It has become almost as socially desirable to have a high I.Q. as a high bust."

Brains have not always been in such high repute. Not long

ago it was considered rather unfortunate if a youngster revealed brilliance at an early age.

In fact, a few months before the end of World War II, a Sunday newspaper supplement published an article entitled, "You're Lucky You're No Genius." Yet at that very time one of history's most concentrated intellectual efforts was being conducted. A group of brilliant men who included some of the finest intellects in the world were perfecting the atomic bomb.

This mass change of heart about the importance of mind has occurred with comparative suddenness. While many educators, scholars, and thoughtful citizens have long been concerned about this country's attitude toward intellectual affairs, most of the public did not become aware of the problem, or concerned with it, until it was startled to learn that the Russians had beaten us to a new technological development. The launching of the first Sputnik can probably be recorded as a major turning point in the American attitude toward the importance of educating the gifted to make the fullest use of their superior abilities. In that sense it can be said that a Russian satellite changed the educational future of millions of American children.

The egghead has been invited to come out of his shell. Educators and psychologists who had long been interested in the plight of the gifted child have found they suddenly have a larger audience than they ever expected. For years they had sighed that it would require an intellectual breakthrough to arouse public concern over the waste of brain power.

The breakthrough has occurred and the public is aroused. Many parents are concerned about what to do for their children if they are gifted. At the same time, many of them still remember the old clichés about child prodigies who become adult failures. Now they hear it isn't so and they wonder what really is the truth about gifted children.

Psychologists and educators have been studying exceptionally bright children for years. These experts have disproved many of the misconceptions about gifted children that for so long were accepted as facts.

A large part of the public has long thought of the gifted child as a little fellow with large glasses who would be bowled over if a baseball were rolled at him. If it were a girl who was gifted, it was presumed she was the kind with whom no boy would want to dance. Gifted children were expected to be undersized, unathletic, unsociable, and inept at doing anything but reading books.

As far as most people were concerned, exceptional intelligence in children not only did not last, but it was advisable to grow out of it as quickly as possible—before the youngster's personality was permanently damaged. The story was frequently told of the boy wonder who entered Harvard at the age of eleven and wound up as a twenty-dollar-a-week clerk whose hobby was collecting streetcar transfers. Few people seemed to consider that the story was told only because this boy was an exception and not the rule. Instead of considering the brilliant children who went on to distinguished adult careers, the highly publicized failure of a few exploited and unfortunate young prodigies who failed to fulfill their promise reinforced the popular prejudice against giftedness.

As further "proof" that brilliant children would probably not become exceptional adults, people recalled the stories told about geniuses of the past who had been considered rather stupid as children. Thomas Edison, for example, was rated practically at the bottom of his class as a youngster. If this were so, it was argued, it seemed obvious that genuine brilliance developed late and gifted children would soon burn themselves out. Accordingly, one might have a better chance of growing into a bright adult if one started out as a slightly dim-witted child.

Those who based their opinion on the great inventor's school record did not know another important fact—the young Edison had read books far beyond his years. Like many other children whose brilliance is not perceived until they achieve fame as adults, the future inventor showed a great deal of talent and initiative while still a child and was encouraged by his mother. But his teachers did not recognize his ability.

In recent years a great deal has been learned about gifted children by closely observing groups of them over a period of years. Hundreds of gifted children, for example, have gone through Hunter College Elementary School since it was started as an experimental school more than fifteen years ago.

The youngest pupils, who attend the nursery school, are three years old. The kindergartners are four to five; those in grades one through six, range in age from five-and-a-half to twelve. The children are admitted to the school on the basis of high intelligence and good physical, social, and emotional development.

They come to the school from many parts of Manhattan and live in all kinds of neighborhoods. Through the years more than fifty ethnic groups have been represented.

Some of the children's parents are well-known public personalities but most are obscure citizens. The families are both poor and well to do. Some parents are native and others are foreign born. From this long, intensive experience with gifted children of varied backgrounds it is possible to draw a composite picture of what the gifted child is really like.

Each child is, of course, very much an individual, with his own interests and personality. Most of the children are simply very intelligent and a few are quite brilliant. Yet, although each child differs from the others, they have certain characteristics and qualities in common.

Visitors often note with surprise how good looking many of the children are. They are healthy, vivacious, and brimming with vitality. As a group they have fewer nervous habits, such as tics or stuttering, than an average group of children would show.

Physically, most of them are better developed than average children. Some are excellent athletes and a few are not up to average, but on the whole they are rarely clumsy or poorly coordinated. The old stereotype of the near-sighted fumbler does not hold true for most gifted children.

Gifted children love to use their minds, but they don't do so self consciously. If they are treated naturally, they accept their intelligence as something ordinary and expected. They are usually surprised to discover that other children are not as bright as they.

Instead of being conceited about their intelligence, they are seldom aware they are exceptional—if their parents have not made the mistake of fussing over them too much. Some of the children, in fact, are not only modest but doubt that they are bright.

Constance, for example, was one of the pleasantest and most helpful children in the school. She got along well with her teachers and her classmates, her schoolwork was good, and she seemed a perfect example of well-adjusted normalcy. Her mother reported that she came home from school one day bubbling with news about Margaret, her best friend. "Margaret knows her I.Q." Constance reported. "It's 136. No wonder she's so bright." What Constance didn't know was that her own I.Q. was 150.

The children almost always have far less knowledge and concern about their test scores than their parents. A questionnaire given to the eleven-year-olds asked: "Do you know what an I.Q. is? If you know your own, write it down. If not, guess." Only two children knew their scores. The rest, having some vague idea that 100 was considered average, estimated their own scores at 100 to 110, although none of them had less than 130. One child defined I.Q. as "Ingenuity

Quiz," a better answer than he realized. Probably the answer that best expressed the children's attitude toward I.Q.'s was, "A test you take to get into Hunter and again to get out."

Like all children, the gifted love to play. All kinds of games and recreational activities interest them. Because they are bright, they are also inventive and imaginative. While they are playing a game they will revise the rules or introduce innovations to make the game more interesting.

Just as gifted children learn more about games and remember more of their rules than average children, their superior memories benefit them in other fields as well. They remember what they are told and therefore they learn quickly. Because their ability to reason and see relationships is superior, they can see more quickly than most children the connection between something they have learned in the past and something they have just found out.

Gifted children often come up with unexpected solutions to everyday problems. Ted's mother came to the school one day to confer with his teacher. She wondered if the teacher could give her the answer to an unimportant but exasperating question. Lately Ted had been insisting he be given exactly the same lunch every day. He wanted three sandwiches, each cut in half, and all containing the same thing— peanut butter, cream cheese, and jelly. Day after day he insisted on the same menu. If his mother tried to vary it, he would argue that it was much easier for her not to have to think up new fillings every day.

"Don't you think it's peculiar for a child to want to eat the same thing every day?" his mother asked. The teacher laughed. She thought that the mothers were in on the six-boy lunch pact. Each of the boys had agreed to come in with three halved sandwiches of the same kind. Between them they therefore had six different kinds of sandwiches and traded around till each had the menu he wanted.

The gifted are not only ingenious, they are also far more

persevering than average children. They will stick to a task and concentrate on it for comparatively long periods of time. The results of their efforts may, of course, sometimes try the good nature of their elders. One day a nursery school teacher at Hunter carefully plugged the bell of a large toy fire engine because it disturbed other classes. However, she did not tell the children what she had done, or why.

Five minutes after the children came out to play with the fire engine, the bell was clanging. One of the children ran over to her and proudly announced, "We looked and looked and found out how to fix it."

Since gifted children are curious, number games and puzzles usually interest them. They love to explore globes, atlases, and encyclopedias. The everyday world fascinates them and they try to learn more about many of the objects that surround them.

The child who eagerly explores special interests and has several hobbies that last for several months or years is likely to be gifted. It is the rare gifted child who has no field of special interest. His interests change, but something specific is almost always absorbing him.

Because the gifted child has far-ranging curiosity, he often develops hobbies that are advanced for children of his age. One eight-year-old was interested in animals and read everything he could about them. He decided he wanted to learn how to stuff them and finally persuaded his mother to let him take a correspondence course in taxidermy.

One day his mother showed up at the school holding a bedraggled-looking pheasant. "I've had a terrible time trying to find one in the city this time of year," she explained. "But Roddy promised to show his class how easy it is to follow the directions in his taxidermy manual."

The gifted are often interested in painting, writing, and music. As will be explained, however, exceptional artistic talent is not necessarily one of the traits of the intellectually gifted. The parent who finds his child busy with paint or clay, or absorbed at the piano, should first consider this interest as a hobby rather than as proof of artistic talent. How a parent can determine if a child has genuine talent, and then help him to develop it, will be discussed in another chapter.

Gifted boys and gifted girls have similar general interests although they usually differ in their specific preferences. Both like to make collections, for example, but as a rule they collect different things.

This is partly because parents and others who influence the child, by considering certain interests "masculine" and others "feminine," help to determine the direction of the children's interests. Little boys are often interested in dolls, for example, but soon outgrow it because they learn it is not the thing in which boys should be interested. Girls, on the other hand, frequently get interested in what are considered boys' hobbies and will often maintain their interest if they receive a little encouragement.

When one class was asked to write about, and illustrate, what the children wanted to be when they grew up, Susan said: "I want to be an archaeologist. I can spell it but I don't know how to draw it."

One of the boys in the class suggested, "All you need to do is to draw a man with very few clothes on, then scatter some bones in the foreground." A thought struck the youngster and he snickered, "But you can't be an archaeologist because girls have to wear a lot."

Susan was undaunted. "Haven't you ever seen a girl in a bikini?"

A precocious sense of humor is a significant sign of giftedness. One eleven-year-old who emerged from a scuffle with a bloody nose commented: "Learning when to duck is an important part of growing up." Since even gifted children, however, are often unaware of the solemnity adults consider appropriate for many occasions, their laughter may sometimes seem inappropriate. Bad puns and hearty appreciation of their own wit are childhood characteristics that may irritate parents, but the ability to see the humor in a situation, recognize absurdities, and use words to create a funny effect are signs of intelligence.

Jimmy had a special talent for taking the measure of his classmates. One boy who was given to a good deal of swagger, arm waving, and boastful gesturing toned down his behavior when Jimmy dubbed him, "Flingo." Another classmate signed his papers with his name and the designation "III" after it. One day Jimmy posted a composition on the bulletin board that he had signed, "Jimmy Kajinsky I."

The capacity for leadership is another sign of giftedness, even though it is difficult to define it and still harder to measure through tests. While a gifted child is not necessarily a leader, a child who is a leader among his playmates is likely to be of superior intelligence. The child who always seems to run things is demonstrating a capacity that is one sign of giftedness.

Barbara always ran her class plays. She wrote the script and saw to it that everybody had a part to play. If somebody was dissatisfied with his role, she found somebody who was willing to trade parts or she added a few lines to make the frustrated actor happy. Instead of taking the leading role for herself, she preferred to run things backstage and make sure the production ran smoothly.

Gifted children will often try to gravitate toward playmates a bit older than themselves if their own age mates can't keep them interested. Acceptance by older children is another sign of above-average development.

Many parents do not recognize that their child has superior abilities because they do not believe he could be gifted. They picture a gifted child as a child prodigy in Eton collar and velvet trousers with a violin tucked under his chin. Their own energetic, athletic, blue-jeaned youngster does not fit this image. They never consider, therefore, that his extensive collections, his interest in puzzles, his unusually large vocabulary, his unending flow of searching questions, his surprisingly adult sense of humor are all signs that his abilities are worth additional attention and cultivation.

While some parents would not be aroused if their child were speaking in sentences before he finished teething, others become excited at each new gurgling syllable. They run to the baby manuals every time a tooth appears to check if it has appeared according to schedule. They are chagrined if the infant does not begin walking until a week after the neighbor's baby manages to stagger his first steps. To such parents each new stage of development is a crisis until it arrives and another proof of baby's brilliance when it is achieved.

As with most complex problems, the proper degree of concern and attention lies between the two extremes. Parents who want to give their child the best opportunities to make the most of his abilities should learn as early as possible what promise their child shows of being gifted. This is sensible and desirable. But parents should not become so overconcerned with the question of giftedness that they become like the mother who wrote in asking how she could administer an I.Q. test to her six-month-old infant.

As will be pointed out in Chapter 3, unless the circumstances are particularly unusual, testing is rarely worthwhile until a child enters school. If a parent feels circumstances do call for special testing, it is best, first, to consult a doctor or psychologist, who will then arrange for testing if he agrees it is needed. But, in most cases where preschool children are concerned, parents should rely primarily on their own observations in order to determine if their child shows signs of giftedness.

The best way to judge whether a baby shows signs of giftedness, therefore, is to observe him carefully. And the first things to observe are such prominent stages of early development as walking and talking. It is important to remember, however, that while early walking and talking are signs of possible giftedness, they are not definitive indications. Some highly gifted individuals did not walk or talk until later than average children usually do.

Babies vary enormously in their individual rate of development. Even the child-development experts differ on the ages that babies are supposed to reach different stages of development. Keep in mind, also, that boys usually develop a bit later than girls. It is impossible, therefore, to lay down hard and fast measurements for determining if the very young child is gifted. In order to keep an accurate record of the baby's development that can be referred to later, procure a "Baby Book" and record the dates as suggested on various pages. Paste in snapshots if space has been provided for them.

The child who walks or talks earlier than most others of the same age and sex shows promising signs of giftedness. However, parents who try to force a child to walk or talk before some imagined deadline do more harm than good.

The baby whose parents hold him up while he wobbles desperately on buckling knees and turned-in ankles does not have his physical development speeded. Nor will his vocabulary be enlarged by dinning words into his head and urging him to repeat them. As Chapters 6 and 7 will explain and illustrate, parents who want to encourage a child to be interested in words, whether for speaking or reading, have to work *with* him, not *on* him.

The way to encourage a child to reveal whatever verbal abilities he may have, is to read to him from books, show him pictures and talk about them with him, and chat with him about the objects that surround his daily life. Speak slowly, enunciate clearly, and avoid "baby talk."

Given these opportunities to learn, a child will be able to demonstrate the extent of his verbal gifts by the manner in which he responds. If he shows a great deal of curiosity about the world around him, an ability to retain what he is told, and a facility for learning new words quickly, he will be showing some of the signs of intellectual giftedness.

While early interest in reading can be a sign of giftedness, too many parents make the error of thinking this is the crucial indicator. A child may or may not learn to read before starting school for reasons that have little to do with his intelligence.

For example, a child who has many playmates and outside interests may have little incentive to learn how to read before starting school. Actually, most of the children who enter Hunter at the nursery school or kindergarten level have not yet learned to read.

Still, if a preschool child does express on his own a strong interest in reading, it is a sign of giftedness. The education column of a national news magazine reported the story of a three-and-a-half-year-old girl who came to her parents and insisted they teach her to read. Her special friends, who were somewhat older, were already in school and she wanted to keep up with them. "I'm so ignorant," she wailed. "I can't stand it."

In general, one of the important ways that parents can judge whether a child shows signs of giftedness is to note what interests him. The child's own choice of activities is one of the most revealing gauges of his giftedness. In addition, the thoroughness with which he explores the activity he is currently engaged in, the extent to which he learns about it, the length of time he concentrates on it—as compared to other children of his age—are means of judging whether the child gives evidence of being gifted.

The differences in interests and in ability to concentrate between gifted and average children is illustrated by one five-year-old who brought her microscope and slides to her kindergarten class. For a few minutes the other children were intrigued by the strange new toy. But after each had peeked through the eyepiece for a few moments they went back to their blocks and their wagons. All except one little boy. He stayed behind and listened attentively while the slides were described and the workings of the microscope explained. The little lady biologist and the newly entranced young man were kindred spirits.

Because of his energy, versatility, and curiosity, the gifted child can often be trying to his parents. He is likely to be impatient with superfluous or inadequate answers, as was the youngster who demanded of his parents, "Don't say 'yes.' Don't say 'no.' Say 'why.'"

When a gifted child has his own views on a subject, it is hard for him to be silent. Often, he will not hesitate to argue in defense of his opinions or take issue with adults. One four-year-old asked his grandmother to tell him a story and was treated to a sugary tale about a "bad little boy" and a "good little boy." At the end he delivered a one-sentence critique: "That's no story, that's an advertisement."

The parents of a gifted child sometimes feel they are being subjected to an unceasing flow of questions. Parents cannot be blamed, and should not blame themselves, if they sometimes shirk explanations and occasionally try not to hear questions.

So far as the children are concerned, however, they are engaged in more than mere chatter. The parents who try to encourage their gifted child to discuss his interests will find that the child usually becomes concerned with philosophical problems and spiritual considerations at an earlier age than most children. Ethical questions, religious matters, and a concern with the meaning of death are perplexities they think about at an earlier age than most children. After the death of an aged neighbor one preschool child came home and asked: "Instead of dying, why don't old people become little children again?"

One six-year-old who overhead his classmates discussing a religious holiday went home and asked, "What is my religion?" His parents, who considered themselves freethinking in religious matters, had planned to explain their viewpoint when the child was older and allow him to select his own faith. Confronted with this question, however, they launched into a hasty explanation of their attitude. The child listened carefully and rendered judgment: "It is very interesting but too mystical." Within the week his parents selected a religious school and enrolled him in an after school program.

The gifted often have a highly developed sense of justice and of right and wrong. One little girl was brought to the school office when she was found disobeying a strict order not to leave the school area. She offered a fairly good excuse for her misconduct, but it was explained that she nevertheless would be penalized because she had committed such a serious breach of the rules. Just then her teacher came in and began offering excuses for her. The child listened to her defender without saying a word. As she was led from the office, she turned back and said, "I believe it's right that I should be punished, for I know the reason for the rule."

Probably the best-known research on what gifted children are like is the pioneering study covering approximately thirty years in the lives of more than fifteen hundred gifted children conducted by Professor Lewis Terman and his associates. A summary of their findings provides a thumbnail sketch of what most gifted children are like and of the kind of adults they will probably grow up to be.

Compared to children of average intelligence, Terman found, most children of the same age in his test group were more advanced in physical development and had fewer physical defects. They were taller and more muscular than the majority of their average playmates. They averaged fewer dental cavities. A smaller percentage of them stuttered or had other speech defects.

The study revealed further that the gifted are usually better behaved, have higher ethical standards, and generally achieve greater personal success than their less intelligent fellows. While it is true that children who show great early promise occasionally fail to fulfill the hopes held out for them, these are the exceptions. The gifted child who leads his classmates in elementary school will probably still be ahead of most of them twenty years later.

Terman's test-group children were rarely the bookworms that gifted children are often suspected of being. Compared to average children of their age, they participated in more extracurricular activities, had more varied interests, more hobbies, and knew more games. The researchers found that a test-group child of nine knew more about different games and their rules than the average twelve-year-old.

As Dr. Terman and his aides continued to study the group while it grew older, they found that still more of the popular beliefs about the gifted were being disproved. Instead of running aground when they matured, most of the group had sailed successfully ahead. Compared to average adults of their age, a smaller number had died, far fewer were alcoholics, or had gotten into trouble with the law. Compared to an average group, a far larger number had gone to college and done well in their studies, and many of the men had substantially higher incomes than the average men of their age.

Some, of course, had failed in their schooling or gotten into personal difficulties, but they were a small minority and there were less of them than an average group would have shown. The point was clear: the lifetime forecast for the gifted child is definitely favorable.

To learn even more of the truth about the gifted, Catherine Cox Miles and several other members of the Terman group made an exhaustive study of the lives of great men of the past. They were most interested in learning about the signs of giftedness that famous men had displayed in childhood. Particular attention was given to men who, though recognized as geniuses in their maturity, had been at some time in their childhood described as backward.

In a number of cases they found that the stories about distinguished men having been considered retarded children were simply not true. In other instances the researchers discovered that while the child may have been considered backward by a teacher or parent who did not recognize his gifts, he was actually showing ample but unrecognized evidence of exceptional ability.

The eighteenth-century poet and playwright, Oliver Goldsmith, had his teacher comment about him, "Never was so dull a boy." Actually he was writing verses at seven and reading Latin poetry at eight. Similarly one of Charles Darwin's teachers turned thumbs down on his intellect. Possibly the real reason the teacher disapproved of him was that the man who developed the theory of evolution from his observations of nature, liked, as a boy, to carry insects and small animals in his pockets.

Dr. Terman and his staff presented ample proof that exceptional intelligence does not spring to life full grown. Other psychologists and educators who have studied the gifted have confirmed Terman's findings. Exceptional intelligence, if given an opportunity to show itself, becomes evident fairly early in a child's life. When giftedness is not noticed, it is usually because parents and teachers do not recognize the signs.

Any description of what gifted children are like has to be based on generalizations made as the result of observing many children. Specific incidents are used to describe what experience has shown to be typical characteristics of the gifted. The result is a group portrait of gifted children in general, not of any one gifted child.

Parents using these descriptions as a guide in judging whether their own child may be gifted should remember that a child is not a type, but an individual. He cannot be evaluated on the basis of whether he matches any single characteristic or incident, but on the over-all quality of his traits and achievements.

A child cannot be placed against a chart that will automatically reveal whether or not he is gifted. Parents should learn to recognize the signs of giftedness, not because it allows them to decide once and for all whether or not their child is gifted, but because it enables them to recognize traits and abilities that are worth encouraging.

The best technique parents can use to help their child reveal his capabilities is to encourage him whenever he makes an effort at a worthwhile new accomplishment and provide him with opportunities to develop a new skill. He will thus have the best chance of developing his own individual gifts so far as he may be able, whether or not he turns out to be "gifted" according to definitions used by psychologists.

CHAPTER TWO

The Meaning of Giftedness

ALTHOUGH PUBLIC INTEREST in the gifted has grown enormously in a comparatively short time, actual knowledge of what the gifted are like and of what giftedness is, lags far behind.

Many parents still share the attitude of the father who was disturbed when told by the school principal that his little girl had exceptional intellectual gifts.

"I don't want her to be a genius," he protested. "I just want her to be a nice, average kid. Won't she outgrow it?"

To this father, as to many parents, giftedness is synonymous with genius. And a genius is thought to be a creature who is strange, possibly a bit sinister, certainly unnatural. In many people's minds anybody who is particularly interested in intellectual activities is a bit abnormal.

There are many who still believe that the best way to handle a child who shows unusual intellectual ability is to ignore him. This attitude toward the gifted child could be summed up as: "If he's really smart, he'll be able to get along on his own. Besides, he'll be better off if he outgrows it and just becomes a normal, well-adjusted child. Most child prodigies grow up to be failures, anyhow."

If more parents knew the truth about gifted children, they would be much more interested in helping their children discover and develop their abilities. Because most people do not realize what intellectually gifted children are really like, they misunderstand and misuse such terms as "gifted," "prodigy," and "genius."

Probably the most misused word of them all is "genius." One popular image of the genius is of someone who isolates himself, preferably in a garret, while he tinkers, paints, or scribbles. Eventually he dies, becomes famous, and a movie is made about him. This might be labeled the old-fashioned genius.

On the other hand, the newspapers are rife with a new kind of genius, either self-described or so labeled by reporters and columnists. The press agent who splashes a movie-queen's picture across the breadth of the country thereby becomes known as a "publicity genius." The advertising executive who can frighten millions of people into buying a new dentifrice gets a reputation as an "advertising genius." The multimillionaire who keeps adding new companies to his collection is deemed a "business genius." And the boy or girl who, for any week, has won the biggest quiz-program prize in television history, is dubbed a "child genius."

Thus there are two pictures of the "genius" in most people's minds. One is an eccentric, the other is a money-maker. Neither conception fits children who are described as being "gifted." Nor do most gifted children fit the popular notion of the child prodigy.

Few children who are considered intellectually gifted are potential Van Goghs, Carnegies, or Mozarts. They are, however, substantially superior to their average age mates in intellectual capacity, most of them are well-adjusted, they would profit greatly from certain special attentions and opportunities, and there is a good chance that, if properly guided, they will achieve a great deal of success, and perhaps even distinction, in their chosen life's work.

These are the children with whom this book is primarily concerned. The first chapter described what they are like. Later there will be a definition of genius as it should be applied to a few children, and their special needs and problems will be discussed. For the present, however, it will be much more useful to know what is meant by intellectual giftedness.

Call a boy or girl gifted today, and the usual picture that comes to mind is of a child who does extremely well in his school work. According to this view, he would be the one who always seems to know the right answers. His homework and test papers presumably get the highest marks. He is the child expected to be at the head of the class, the one whom other pupils label "the brain."

Although most people think giftedness means intellectual superiority demonstrated by outstanding work in the classroom, the current definition of giftedness used by psychologists and educators covers a greater variety of abilities than those necessary just to do outstanding school work. Besides, gifted children are, unfortunately, not always found at the head of the class.

So far as meeting the demands of his schoolwork are concerned, the gifted child may find he has too much of a good thing. The work may be too easy. The teacher probably has little time for his special needs because she has to devote most of her attention to those children who cannot keep up. The very qualities that make a child gifted, such as his curiosity, his imagination, his quick comprehension of new material, may make the classroom seem dull and uninteresting. In such cases, if his home environment does not give him adequate opportunities for the development and use of his superior abilities, he may find his outlets by getting in the teacher's hair instead of on her honor roll.

An important step in the successful handling of gifted children, therefore, is to understand what comprises giftedness. Then one can learn how to develop it, how to lead it into constructive channels, and how to cope with the problems that a child sometimes faces just because he is gifted.

In order to decide whether a child is gifted, it is first necessary to know what is meant when a teacher or a psychologist speaks of "giftedness." The term giftedness is most often used to describe exceptional intellectual ability, as distinct from talent.

Intellectual ability is not a single entity. It is actually a group of skills. Different gifted children possess each of these skills in different degrees. Intellectual ability should therefore be thought of as a tool kit, rather than a single tool, and as a kit in which some of the tools may be of better quality than others.

Some of the most important tools in the "kit" known as intellectual ability are:

1. *Verbal Skill.* This skill has two parts—first, the ability to comprehend written or spoken material and second, the ability to use words effectively in speaking or writing. Gifted children have a high degree of skill in verbal comprehension, since they are good learners. They will not necessarily be especially talented writers or speakers, although they will probably be above average in their ability to express themselves.

Children with verbal skill amass large vocabularies. They not only understand more words than average children, but can express themselves more skillfully in speaking and writing. They are often good readers who can absorb rapidly printed matter considered too difficult for their age group.

How children differ in their level of skill in understanding and using words is illustrated by an incident that took place in a nursery school class. The teacher overheard a three-year-old using improper language. Drawing the little girl over to her, the teacher asked if she knew the meaning of the words. The little girl shook her head. "I wouldn't use words I didn't understand," the teacher suggested. "They might not be proper."

A little boy who had overheard the conversation piped up. "I think I know what you mean. It's all right to say, *oui, oui* in French, but it's not good in English."

This little boy had both kinds of verbal skill. His vocabulary included a French phrase beyond the comprehension of most American children his age and he could use his knowledge of words to make a point with special effectiveness.

2. *Numerical Skill.* This is the ability to handle ideas that are expressed by numbers. Children with this skill are more than simply good at doing the basic operations of adding, subtracting, multiplying, and dividing. They can perceive the relationships between numbers. They have a special aptitude for understanding the meaning of the idea being expressed when a mathematical symbol is used. Those who have a high degree of numerical skill, such as theoretical physicists, can think by using mathematical symbols in the same way that others think with words.

Many children who later become scientists show an early interest in numbers and an aptitude for using them. A good illustration of the way a child with a high degree of numerical skill thinks about numbers is the story told about the five-year-old who excitedly reported to his father a discovery he had made. He had figured out that the number 2520 could be divided by every number from one through ten.

3. *Spatial Skill.* This is the ability to understand how parts of things fit together. For example, a globe divided into irregular pieces and diagrammed on a flat sheet of paper can be visualized as an entity only if one has a fair amount of spatial skill. Architects must have spatial skill, since they must visualize in their minds how a building will look from

different points of view. This requires the ability to think in three dimensions.

When a drawing of an object divided into its parts is shown to a child with a high degree of spatial skill, he will be especially good at figuring out how it should be put together. These children are often talented at interpreting diagrams when they work with construction toys.

4. *Reasoning Skill.* This skill, sometimes called logical ability, is also considered to be made up of several parts. For the purpose of this simplified analysis, these can be described as the ability to make plans on the basis of known facts, to learn from past experience, to foresee the consequences of a particular course of action; the ability to figure out what sequence of incidents led up to a particular occurrence (the kind of deductive reasoning found, for example, in detective stories); and the ability to find the relationship between seemingly separate and unrelated facts or events (the way new scientific theories are developed from individual bits of research).

On a simple level, the baby who burns himself at the stove and then, without specific warning, avoids the barbecue pit, is doing some good logical reasoning for his age. He has been able to figure out the relationship and the similarity between two apparently different and separate things.

Another example of a child displaying exceptional reasoning power for his age, by anticipating a problem and figuring out in advance how to solve it, was demonstrated by a nine-year-old. This boy devised a system for handling the numerous thank you notes that his parents made him write each year after receiving his Christmas presents. His parents were amazed when he announced the day after Christmas that all his letters had gone out. Later they learned that long before Christmas he had prepared a set of form letters with blank spaces for the name of the sender and the gift. As soon as the presents were opened, the blank spaces were filled in.

Intellectual ability can be broken down into additional components and described in still other ways. For example, children with unusually vivid imaginations are often exceptionally bright. A good memory is often a sign of intelligence, although the so-called photographic memory may simply be a freak ability rather than a sign of brilliance.

Psychologists have developed many different lists of what they consider the most important intellectual skills. Those that have been outlined are the intellectual skills that parents will recognize most easily. The child who is well above average in at least several of these skills is probably intellectually gifted.

A gifted child does not have the same degree of superiority in every intellectual skill. He may be above average in all of them, but outstanding in one or two. One child may be especially good at numbers, another particularly adept with words, and so on.

In addition to being intellectually gifted, a child may also have other important abilities. Blended together with some of the intellectual gifts already described, he may then have outstanding artistic or mechanical talent. A superior capacity for creative thinking in any field—for example, science—is not generally considered as a separate intellectual skill. Rather, it is a particular blending of intellectual skills and specialized interests that produces a specific kind of giftedness.

Many parents mistakenly think a child who is intellectually gifted will be equally gifted in such other areas as music and art. It is valuable, therefore, to gain some understanding of the specific abilities that make up different kinds of giftedness. For example, parents have been disappointed because their intellectually gifted child could not play a musical instrument well. They did not realize that no matter how intelligent he is, he may have poor rhythmic sense, a defective ear for pitch, or other failings that would keep him from becoming an outstanding musician.

Intellectual gifts must be accompanied by certain physical gifts in order to produce genuine artistic talent. This is why psychologists and educators emphasize that, while intellectually gifted children are frequently interested in different forms of artistic expression, outstanding artistic talent is far more rare.

To understand the reason for this, think of artistic giftedness as a combination of certain superior intellectual skills—plus certain additional abilities.

The novelist, for example, needs excellent verbal ability and imagination plus an unusual type of psychological insight.

The painter must have a highly developed sense of spatial relationships and sensitivity to colors.

A dancer must have a good memory plus the physical skills of both the musician and the athlete.

These examples illustrate two points parents should keep in mind:

1. Almost all gifted children share certain basic characteristics. At the same time, children express their giftedness in widely different ways. No matter what their specifically outstanding talents may be, almost all gifted children have in common the fact that they are superior in the basic intellectual abilities. The budding writer, the potential scientist, the future painter are especially gifted in a particular area of giftedness. At the same time they all are, even though to different degrees, intellectually superior. This explains why almost all artistically talented children are above average, even though only a small number of intellectually gifted children also have outstanding artistic talent.

2. Children show different kinds of giftedness in differing degrees. The parent trying to understand the nature of his child's giftedness should be concerned not only with the

kind of gift the child shows, but also with the amount of giftedness he displays.

Gifted children need a degree of stimulation appropriate to their capacities. We have all seen examples of the two basic errors parents make when they have a mistaken estimate of their children's ability.

Some parents think their children far less able than they really are and stifle their abilities—like the father who brushes off the early, comparatively crude efforts of a youngster who shows promise of becoming a fine painter. This parent's mistake lies in not realizing how far beyond other children his child's work proves him to be.

On the other hand, some parents think their children are far more capable than happens to be the case and make impossible demands of them—like the mother who insists on making a concert violinist out of a child who could learn to play agreeably, but lacks the special muscular co-ordination which prevents him from becoming a virtuoso.

In trying to set up standards for recognizing different degrees of giftedness in children, educators usually make a distinction between "extremely gifted" and "gifted" children. They also distinguish between "intellectually gifted" children and "talented" children.

No firm rules define different kinds and amounts of intellectual, artistic, and other abilities, and not all educators and psychologists interested in this field use the same definitions in quite the same way. Still, it will make discussion of the whole subject easier if we explain the generally accepted categories into which superior children are classified.

To be placed in the broad category of "gifted," a child has to show a substantial degree of intellectual superiority. The generally accepted standard for intellectual giftedness is considered to be anywhere from the top one to five per cent of the child's age group. In terms of intelligence quotients, which will be discussed in the next chapter, this usually includes I.Q.'s of 130 and above.

"Extremely gifted" is the top category of intellectual giftedness. While "gifted" may be considered to include anywhere from one to five children in a hundred, the "extremely gifted" child has been described as the one child in a hundred thousand who, as an adult, may deserve to be called a "genius."

A child who is considered gifted in some particular field is usually intellectually superior in general. Then, the specific vocational direction toward which his individual blend of gifts and interests leads him will cause him to be considered scientifically gifted, mechanically gifted, artistically gifted, and so on.

Other children, who are not sufficiently superior to be thought of as intellectually gifted, may still have special abilities that certainly deserve to be encouraged and cultivated. These children are usually described as being "talented." The child who sings, plays a musical instrument, draws, or makes things with his hands in a way that shows him to be superior to his age mates is obviously "talented" even if, technically, he is not considered intellectually gifted.

The reason for making a distinction between talented children and gifted children is to allow for the difference between the child who is skillful and the child who is creative. The I.Q. is accepted as an indicator of potential creativity because, in general, those who distinguish themselves in creative achievement also have a high degree of intellectual ability.

The most important indicators of giftedness in adults are creativity and originality. These are the marks of the true artist, scientist, business and political leader, inventor. We evaluate a genius by how much he creates and by how original he is in the work he produces. In children, the difference between talent and giftedness is, on the whole, the difference in potential creativity.

When a parent thinks of talent and giftedness as yardsticks for estimating a child's potential creativity, he then has a guide for estimating his child's capacity for achievement. And it then becomes apparent why it is usually meaningless to call even the highly gifted child a "genius."

Genius signifies someone who has shown extraordinary creative achievement. Rarely does even the most highly gifted child demonstrate this kind of ability while still young. Genuine child prodigies are few and far between.

Mozart, composing waltzes and making concert tours at six; the philosopher John Stuart Mill, reading Greek at three; the painter Van Dyck, with his own pupils at sixteen, may reasonably be called child geniuses.

Compare these extraordinary achievements with even the most unusual accomplishments of most of the highly gifted children whom the newspapers momentarily dub "child prodigies" and you begin to understand the wide range of ability and accomplishment that is included in the broad category of giftedness.

This does not mean that only those children who come close to proving themselves to be authentic child prodigies will become brilliantly creative adults. Great creative achievement, including that height of originality we call genius, begins to manifest itself at different ages, depending on the individual and the field in which he is expressing his gifts.

No matter how precocious a gifted child may be, he usually needs to be fairly mature before he can achieve genuine creative originality. It takes a certain amount of time before one can learn enough about what others have done to be able to go ahead and do something new. To go back to an example offered before, we do not remember Mozart because he composed little waltzes at six; we remember the waltzes he composed so early because they are a forerunner of the great works he later produced.

Physicists and mathematicians often produce much of their most important creative work while they are still in their twenties. Norbert Wiener, a child prodigy who entered college at twelve, became a brilliant mathematician, and one of the most important figures in the development of electronic brains, points out:

"Mathematics and physics are known as a young man's game. They involve the athleticism of the intellect and constitute a field in which power and *élan* are more valuable than massed experience. There are exceptions, but it is a safe general rule that, if a mathematician has not made his mark by the time he is thirty, the betting is strongly against his ever making a significant mark at any later time."

The same is usually true of poets. Mathematics and poetry are both fields in which the flash of insight, the imaginative combination of previously unrelated ideas are most important. Albert Einstein, Niels Bohr, John von Neumann are only a few of the famous modern physicists and mathematicians who made important contributions to their fields while still in their early twenties. John Keats and Percy Bysshe Shelley are two of the most famous examples of how early the talent for lyric poetry flowers.

But in fields where personal experience and an understanding of human relationships are important, even the most precocious child must wait before he can begin to produce important work. The novelist, the historian, particularly the statesman, because of the nature of what they do, almost always need more time. Alexander the Great was able to demonstrate his military genius while still in his teens because his father was king and could give him an army. Although John Stuart Mill was one of the most intellectually precocious boys in history, he did not write his important philosophical works until he was a grown man. Instrumental prodigies, such as Heifetz, though they perform extraordinarily well as children, need to mature before they become capable of true interpretive artistry.

For parents, therefore, the great challenge presented by their child's abilities, no matter whether they turn out to constitute talent or giftedness, is, first, to gain an understanding of how much potential achievement they promise and, then, to help provide the means for the promise to be fulfilled.

CHAPTER THREE

How to Discover Giftedness

NOBODY CAN TRY to explain giftedness without explaining the meaning of the two-letter abbreviation that has become the best-known—and most misunderstood—expression in all of psychology. The two letters are "I.Q." Spelled out, they stand for intelligence quotient.

As well-known as intelligence tests and I.Q. scores have become, most people still misunderstand the test's purpose and the score's meaning. For adults, the I.Q. represents a comparison between the individual who has just been tested and the rest of the adult population. In the case of a child, his I.Q. is a comparison between his intelligence and the intelligence of what psychologists consider the average child of his age. The six-year-old with an I.Q. of 100 theoretically has the same intelligence as the average six-year-old.

Actually, two children with the same I.Q. can differ completely in personality, in aptitudes, and in the various characteristics that are so important for successful living. The I.Q., as this chapter will explain, tells something about a child, but it does not tell enough about him. And many parents are too concerned with I.Q.'s for their children's good.

Intelligence tests are based on approximations and averages. They have been worked out during the past fifty years by psychologists who have developed standards of what the average child at different ages, and the average adult, should be able to accomplish when faced with problems intended to test his intellectual abilities.

The modern intelligence test was created by the French psychologist, Alfred Binet, who tried out his first tests on Paris school children in 1905. Binet worked out standards of what a three-year-old should know, what a four-year-old should know, and so on. These early tests have since been revised and refined by many other psychologists. The Stanford-Binet test and similar intelligence tests are based on the same principle. The score of the person tested is compared to the average standard of achievement for his age group and this comparison is then stated in the form of an I.Q. number.

To understand how a child's I.Q. number is determined, merely remember that it is based on a comparison between two scales—the age of the child in actual years, and the child's mental age as shown by his score on the intelligence test. To derive the I.Q., his mental age is divided by his chronological age. Since the resulting number would usually contain a fraction, it is multiplied by one hundred to make it easier to express. The answer is the intelligence quotient, or I.Q.

To derive the I.Q. of a child of six whose achievement on an intelligence test is equivalent to that of a nine-year-old, divide his mental age (9) by his chronological age (6). Multiply the result (1½) by 100. You then have the child's I.Q. —150. Had this child shown a mental age of six, his I.Q. would be 100. Simply stated, the child's I.Q. is a comparison between his chronological age and his mental age.

The first question that usually comes to parents' minds when they learn their children have been given intelligence tests is: "How does my child compare with his classmates?"

One veteran teacher, who has faced this question from many parents, remarked: "Tell parents their child's vision is slightly below normal 20/30 and they are concerned for him; tell them the child's I.Q. is a normal 99 and they are indignant with you." Most parents are satisfied to have their children considered average as long as they believe they are really slightly above average.

In general, I.Q. categories are described as follows:

130 I.Q. and above—"gifted"

120-129 I. Q.—"very bright"

110-119 I.Q.—"bright"

90-109 I.Q.—"average"

On the whole, an I.Q. of about 120 is considered necessary to do good work in the leading colleges. Most of the grade schools that offer special classes for the gifted require an I.Q. of 130, but many make special provisions for pupils with I.Q.'s of 120 or above.

It is a mistake to set a specific number at which any category begins. The only excuse for doing it is to have some boundary with which to define broad groups or to set a minimum grade for admission to limited facilities.

At Hunter College Elementary School, for example, many more capable children apply than can be accepted. Therefore, one of the requirements for admission is an I.Q. of at least 130. This does not mean, however, that while a child of 130 I.Q. is gifted, a child of 129 I.Q. automatically is not. Human beings in general, and children particularly, are much too varied to fit into rigid groupings. In addition, any I.Q. score is expected to have a possible error of about 5 points. A child who scores 130 on a Stanford-Binet test may actually have an I.Q. between 127 and 133.

A great deal has been written about the comparative importance of heredity and environment in determining intelligence. Most psychologists agree that both are important. Heredity determines the ceiling of a child's ability. This is his inborn capacity to learn. Environment determines how much of this innate potential is developed and used. Many psychologists have become convinced that most children have a great deal more inborn ability than they use. Thus, no matter what a child's I.Q. may be, if he gets the benefits of his parents' attention and encouragement he will probably accomplish a good deal more than a child with greater natural gifts whose abilities are neglected.

As a distinguished psychologist once said, "Only talent turned to achievement means anything." It is the parent's task to inspire his child to achieve and help him learn how to do so.

The best advice, therefore, that can be given to parents who compare their child's I.Q. to other children's is: stop doing it. Leave the comparative scoring to the psychologists. Your concern is your individual child and his individual needs. Your interest in his I.Q. should not be based on how high it is, but on what it indicates regarding the kind of learning opportunities he needs.

Although the I.Q. is valuable to professional psychologists as a guide, too many laymen think of it as an infallible prophet. As a result, not only do parents usually misunderstand the meaning of the I.Q., they are also misled by it. They are not aware of the important qualities that the intelligence test does not measure. The person possessing these traits to an unusual degree may accomplish far more in life than his I.Q. score alone would lead one to expect. For their children's sake, therefore, parents should not make the mistake of thinking the I.Q. tells all.

At least as important as sheer intellectual ability, for example, are certain character traits that an intelligence test does not measure. We have all known children who showed enormous promise—but never fulfilled it. They never seemed to finish anything they started. Usually they lacked the will power, the sense of direction, and the desire to succeed necessary to carry them through the inevitable effort and disappointment that even the most capable child must face in the course of developing and training his gifts.

Unless accompanied by motivation to learn and achieve, gifts will lose much of their value, for they will never be developed to their potential maximum. As one psychologist has put it, "The I.W. or 'I will' is more important than the I.Q." A child's future is as much determined by his character as by his intellect.

In addition to character traits, a variety of aptitudes are comparatively untested by an intelligence test. A creative artist, for example, cannot reveal his gifts on such a test. Although a fine painter or musician is likely to have a high I.Q., his score might very well be matched by someone who will never approach him in creative achievement. Creativity is best revealed by what it creates. Future success in any field requiring exceptional individuality and imagination cannot be predicted on the basis of an I.Q. score.

The special combination of personal magnetism, energy, and psychological insight that results in the capacity for leadership is similarly unmeasurable by an intelligence test. In fields such as politics and business administration, the man who has this capacity for leadership will probably go much further than the man without it who may have even a ten-point higher I.Q.

What does all this signify for most parents? It is worth stressing again that the parent who worries about his child's exact I.Q. score and is disturbed because it may be three points lower than the I.Q. of the neighbor's child, who is six months younger, is concerned with the wrong problem. Such a parent is very much like the test-happy parent who has his child repeatedly tested in an effort to have him achieve a more satisfying score. Both parents are paying more attention to their own vanity than their children's needs.

The proper home environment is what children need most

for the maximum development of their inborn capacity. If children are not to be stunted either physically or mentally, they need the proper nutrition for both their bodies and their minds. Just as a child requires good food right from infancy in order to grow properly, so does he need a suitable early environment for good mental development.

Most children have skills that are worth encouraging and developing. Since the general principles for the development of giftedness could be profitably applied to almost all children, the parent's main concern should not be with his child's exact position on the I.Q. scale, but with helping him attain the level of achievement his various aptitudes promise.

What a child needs most from his parents in order to develop his innate abilities to their highest possible level is the encouragement, the discipline, and the opportunities that together result in the two essentials for intellectual achievement—strong motivation to learn and self-discipline. Nothing contributes more toward their development than proper home environment. Providing this environment, and thus giving a youngster the incentive for achievement, is the best contribution parents can make to the development of their children's capacities.

Do not expect tests to tell you all about your child. Tests are not as reliable as parents think. The experts themselves treat tests with more skepticism and caution than laymen. Sometimes a child may score ten points lower on a group intelligence test given in the classroom than he does later on a test that a trained psychologist administers to him individually. The best-known tests have to be given to individual children by a trained tester. Most schools, however, do not have the facilities to test this way.

The tests that are used to measure specific aptitudes are even less reliable. The value of many of the tests used to determine artistic and other creative abilities is still being debated by psychologists. Often they test only some of the skills needed to do well in a particular field. A test for artistic aptitude, for example, may test a child's sense of design but not his color sense.

On the whole, aptitude tests have been only moderately reliable when given to adults. They are even less dependable when given to children, whose skills are still comparatively unformed, although research is in progress to improve these measurements.

The usual tests of classroom work a child takes may show how well he stands in his class, but can be a poor indicator of his actual abilities. As will be shown later, this can be particularly true if the child is exceptionally gifted.

One of the reasons that it is important for parents to understand the purpose and value of intelligence and aptitude tests is to enable them to understand why they should place *less* reliance on testing and more on their own well-informed observation of their children. Many parents are eager for their children to be tested even before they have finished teething. Often they would like to do the testing themselves, as did the mother who wrote in asking where to buy an I.Q. test for her six-month-old infant.

A mother can tell by her baby's behavior whether he is normal. If she insists on knowing exactly how bright he is, it is to please herself, not for the baby's good. There will be time enough to test him—if it is necessary—when he is old enough to express himself. The very young child is unable to make the specific, detailed responses necessary for accurate intelligence testing. On the whole, unless testing is recommended by someone such as a nursery-school teacher or a doctor, there is little point in his being tested before he enters school.

How, then, should a parent try to determine whether his child shows genuine signs of being gifted or talented in a specific field? A child should be observed at work and at play. The opinions of others should be taken into account.

Tests can then be used at the proper time to measure the extent of abilities that have been observed, or, sometimes, to reveal unsuspected abilities in children who lacked opportunities to explore and express their interests.

Since actual performance is the best test of all, the best way to judge whether a child has specific aptitudes is to observe how well he does in different fields. As an example, let us take sports, where fathers often do serve as aptitude testers.

If a father wants to know if his nine-year-old has enough talent to be a Little League baseball pitcher, he doesn't start by having him tested for visual acuity, muscular strength, and memory of baseball rules. He hands him a baseball, picks up a mitt, and tells him to throw. If the ball comes in fast and straight, father decides it is worth trying to teach him how to throw a curve. If the boy continues to show an aptitude for pitching, father probably takes him off to the Little League coach for an expert opinion. Of course, the boy's own preference would also be important in determining what position he should play.

Several points should be kept in mind by parents when they attempt to judge their child's aptitudes. In the example we have been using, the father's own knowledge of baseball —gained from having played himself, from watching young players, and from having seen how experts play—gives him good standards of comparison. He does not expect his potential Little Leaguer to be able to strike out teen-agers. If the boy can get the ball past other children his age, he is recognized as being talented. If he even manages to strike out a few older boys, father realizes he may be a gifted pitcher.

The same techniques apply to observing and judging all aptitudes. Whenever possible, the whole skill should be tested by actual performance. When this cannot be done, tests are used to explore as many as possible of the specific skills that make up the total aptitude. To judge the quality of the aptitude being demonstrated, one must have personal experience and knowledge of the particular field. It is also important not to expect adult levels of achievement even from youngsters who are gifted.

The decision as to whether a child is gifted cannot be based on any one test and certainly not on a single, nonprofessional opinion. Parents may recognize signs of giftedness, but they are usually not experienced enough to evaluate accurately their observations. In most cases a parent cannot judge the degree of aptitude a child shows unless the parent is expert in music, mechanics, or any other field in which the child is interested and shows promise.

The parent's assignment—and it is the most important responsibility of all—is to give the child opportunities to explore various fields, note which of them the child finds particularly interesting, and then allow him to explore them more fully. If the child appears to be making rapid progress in a particular field, it may then be desirable to have an expert appraise his work.

Giftedness is often discovered in the classroom. Good schools have testing programs to explore their pupils' intellectual ability and their aptitudes. Experienced teachers have a continuing opportunity to observe each child's work and note whatever outstanding abilities each may demonstrate.

On the other hand, schoolwork may cause a child to hide his giftedness. If the work is too far below the level of his ability, he may grow bored, neglect it, and therefore appear not able to do it. Sometimes, children are embarrassed by the remarks of their fellow pupils if they show too much knowledge. In order not to be the butt of remarks about being "brains" and gibes about using "big words," they may prefer to hide their knowledge and not reveal their abilities.

Some teachers are poor judges of giftedness, for it is easier to think highly of a well-behaved child who does his work without creating any bother, than of a child who is restless, questioning, and perhaps acts mischievously out of sheer boredom. The first child may actually be pleasant and average, while the second is annoying but bright.

Children's evaluations of their fellows are often used as a test of the social adjustment and personality characteristics of the members of the group. Children can be very good judges of other children's skills, such as aptitude for leadership. If a child's playmates seek his opinion and his leadership, it is probably because he has demonstrated the ability to run things well.

Children also acknowledge the brighter members of their class or play group, even when they may not like them. They can accept with more equanimity than their parents the fact that some pupils receive A's on their report cards in contrast to their own B's or C's.

In the final analysis, giftedness is something that has to be proven as much as discovered. Fortunately, persistence is one of the most important traits of the gifted. If given a reasonable chance, the gifted child will, himself, prove he is gifted. But parents should provide the opportunities and be able to recognize the evidence.

Check List: Is Your Child Gifted?

Most, but not all, of the following questions apply equally well to children of various ages. They are intended to serve as a check list of the abilities revealed by many gifted children and not as an actual test that will pinpoint whether a child is gifted.

Although there is no score that indicates giftedness, parents who can answer "yes" to most of the questions can be fairly sure their child is gifted.

1. Did your child walk and talk earlier than most other children of his age and sex?

2. Did he show a comparatively early interest in words?

3. Does he have an exceptionally large vocabulary for his age?

4. Did he show an early interest in reading?

5. Did he show an early interest in clocks, calendars, jigsaw puzzles?

6. Did he show an early interest in numbers?

7. Does he express curiosity about many things?

8. Does he have more stamina and strength than other children of his age and sex?

9. Does he tend to associate with children older than himself?

10. Does he act as a leader among children of his own age?

11. Does he have a good memory?

12. Does he show unusual reasoning power?

13. Does he have an unusual capacity for planning and organizing?

14. Does he relate information gained in the past to new knowledge that he acquires?

15. Does he show more interest in creative effort and new activities than in routine and repetitive tasks?

16. Does he try to excel in almost everything he does?

17. Does he concentrate on a single activity for a prolonged period without getting bored?

18. Does he usually have a number of interests that keep him busy?

19. Does he persist in his efforts in the face of unexpected difficulties?

20. Does he figure out his own solutions to problems and show uncommon "common sense?"

21. Does he have a sense of humor that is advanced for his age?

22. Does he show sensitivity to the feelings of others?

23. Does he show a comparatively early interest in God, religion, and questions of right and wrong?

24. Does he make collections that are more advanced or unusual than those of others in his age group?

25. Does he show an intense interest in some artistic activity, such as drawing, singing, dancing, writing, playing a musical instrument?

26. Does he make up stories that are vivid and dramatic or relate his experiences with a great deal of exact detail?

27. Does he like puzzles and various kinds of "problem" games?

28. Does he have exceptional ability in mathematics?

29. Does he show an unusual interest in science or mechanics?

30. Does he show awareness of things that are new or novel?

Part II

HOW TO BE A GIFTED PARENT

CHAPTER FOUR

The Right Approach to Giftedness

"DESPITE ALL the concern over gifted children," the young mother of an exceptionally bright little girl commented, "not much attention is being paid to the effort you have to make in order to be a gifted child's parent. Just as important as the many things you're supposed to do," she continued, "are the things you should avoid doing and the advice from so many friends that you have to ignore."

Most parents who have successfully weathered the job of raising an exceptionally intelligent child know that one has to be a gifted parent in order to do a good job. And, as the young mother pointed out, a large part of the task consists of knowing what not to do as well as what to do.

Considering all the instructions and criticisms about education that are filling the air, the most positive piece of advice one can give the conscientious and concerned parent is: stop worrying! The spate of psychoanalytical movies and television dramas about adults whose lives have been ruined by childhood experiences has left some parents fearful that any misstep can ruin their youngster's future. When such parents find their child is gifted, they fear that his psyche is especially delicate, and they become even more worried.

So it's worth repeating. Don't worry every time you encounter a problem in child rearing. Every child has had to face these problems, most of them turn out pretty well, and the odds are even better if your child is gifted. So relax. Raising a gifted child is an interesting challenge. It does make extra demands of the parent who wants to do the best job he can for his child. But don't view the raising of a gifted child as a frightening steeplechase in which, if you stumble over one obstacle, your child will be thrown permanently out of the race.

Keep in mind that most children are pretty hardy and durable, and gifted children are usually even more so than the average. Their lives will not be ruined by one frustration. Besides, a certain amount of frustration is unavoidable, and even desirable. Of course, there are certain social and emotional problems that gifted children are likely to encounter as a consequence of being gifted. But if they have been well directed during their early years, they will have the inner resources to meet these problems and overcome them. Part of your job will be to help them develop this inner strength.

Parents may try to protect their children from the normal buffeting that comes from having to put up with other people and from moving about in the everyday world. They should remember that this is a part of the learning process to which gifted children in particular have to be exposed just because they may have problems in learning how to handle other people. They must share the daily experiences of average children in order to learn how to get along in the everyday world.

An example of a parent who did not realize this is the mother who brought her child for an interview in the kindergarten and carried her five-year-old in her arms the entire morning. With this kind of care he was not ready to stand on his own in school, although his I.Q. was very high. The parents of the gifted child should therefore make it their objective, not to wrap him in a protective cocoon, but to help him to deal successfully with the stresses every human being must endure as he grows up. Worth keeping in mind is the following guide suggested by one writer, who declared that, "A child is being well educated when it is being made more and more independent of the parent."

A parent cannot understand his child until he has some understanding of himself and of his own feelings. Every child has some failings and so does every parent. The parent who is aware of his own weaknesses can then help his child to gain emotional strength.

Any parent who has read this far is interested in doing the best by his child and his gifts. He knows, in general terms, the kind of parent he wants to be—understanding, informed, helpful, constructive. He knows the kind of parent he does not want to be—fearful, domineering, overprotective, over-demanding. How, then, can the parent check on himself to learn if he is reasonably successful at being the kind of parent who will contribute the most to his child's development?

Parents can begin by checking their own attitude toward their child's giftedness. For example, how does he react to the fact that his child may be brighter than himself?

He probably is proud of it and hopeful that the youngster will turn out to be as bright as he seems. But it is not unnatural or unexpected for parents to be a little fearful of what their children may think of them if they do not have the child's capacity for intellectual achievement. Or, they may be self-conscious because they do not have as much formal education as they think they need in order to provide the best opportunities for a gifted child.

This is not the same problem as that of the parent who actually resents his child's giftedness. Such parents resist efforts to have their child given enriched learning opportunities, they brush off suggestions that their child would benefit from certain activities. They may claim that they do not want the child to be "different" from his brothers and sisters, as one family insisted. He was probably too bright for his own good, they said, and they weren't going to be responsible for his getting any brighter.

Such parents often get their way. The child who is denied a chance to develop his mind is in the same dilemma as the child whose body never gets sufficient opportunity to grow and strengthen because he cannot get out enough and use his muscles.

One school found it necessary to devise a way of helping a child hide the truth about his giftedness from his parents and friends. Not only had his playmates begun to look on him suspiciously, but even his parents viewed his exceptional school record with disfavor. So the teacher prepared two report cards. The boy's actual grades, almost all A's, went on the school records; a second report, made up of respectable C's, went home to his family.

More common than parents who actually resent their child's superior abilities are those parents who fear that their child, being "different," must necessarily be unhappy as a consequence. Such parents believe the best way to insure a reasonably secure future for their child is to make the child, as one father put it, "as much as possible like everybody else." When this family learned that their girl had unusual talent for painting, they insisted stubbornly that she take business courses and drop her artistic interests. They wanted her, they said, to learn some "practical" skills for her own good. The girl gave in to her parents and became a mediocre bookkeeper, wistfully recalling the opportunities she had been denied.

But such parents would not even be concerned about identifying giftedness. What about the parent who believes his child is gifted and is concerned as to whether he, himself, has the background and ability to cope with it?

What such a parent needs is reassurance. He should remember that every child, no matter how gifted, is first of all a child. He has a child's emotions and therefore needs sympathetic and understanding parents more than he needs sophisticated, intellectual mentors. Such parents will help their child find the knowledge he craves. They will give him the support and encouragement that will enable him to overcome obstacles and learn how to make the best use of his gifts. They will teach him the principles of living that he needs to learn in order to become a happily functioning person. While academic knowledge can be gathered from many sources, the emotional and social adjustment that comes only from being loved, and from being happily aware of it, must be acquired at home.

Parents should not fear that their own lack of schooling will lose them their gifted child's regard or make them incapable of meeting his wants. Their child's primary desire is for their affection, approval, and assistance. Knowing this, parents will then have the confidence to meet the other needs created by their child's giftedness.

Parents who are interested in doing a bit of self-study so that they can understand their child better and handle him more effectively should first check to see whether they are too demanding of the child. Often the parents of gifted children, used to their quick responses and sometimes seemingly adult intelligence, will make the mistake of dealing with gifted children as if they really are adults.

One five-year-old girl had the regular assignment of setting the table for family meals, a fairly demanding task in itself. Her mother stepped out to the store one afternoon while the lunch soup was warming on the stove and little Jean was setting the table. When she came back a few minutes later, the table was set, the soup was poured—and some of it was spilled on the tablecloth. Instead of praising the unusual effort, mother's first remark was, "Who spilled the soup?"

Unexpectedly, Jean denied doing it. When her mother

proved that nobody else could have done it, the youngster
reluctantly confessed.

"Why did you fib?" her mother asked. The answer finally
brought home to her mother the truth about her unapprecia-
tive nagging. "Because," the little girl explained, "I'm tired
of hearing you always say, 'Oh, Jean!'"

As was pointed out before and will be pointed out again,
the gifted child is, first of all, a child and only, secondly,
gifted. He is not an adult in a small body and he should not
be treated like one. Those parents who exploit their children's gifts are forcing them to forfeit the delights of childhood. They give them the responsibilities of adults while
they still have only the capabilities of children.

Most parents of gifted children know enough nowadays
not to exploit their children as some child prodigies of the
past were exploited. The youthful musician who is taken on
prolonged and strenuous concert tours, as if he were already an adult artist, the mathematical wizard who is put on
display at evening parties and treated like a curiosity are
encountered rarely. Most exploitation of gifted children is
of a different kind and most parents who do it are not even
aware of it.

The kind of child exploitation of which the parents of a
gifted child have to be careful is that which takes the form
of demanding more of the child than his age warrants, even
though he is gifted. Somebody once commented that no
child is born civilized. They all have to be trained to live in
a civilized society. Some parents make the mistake of thinking gifted children need not be taught the same things as
average children. They forget that every child has to be
taught to get along with other children, to be generous, to be
honest, to be obedient, and, above all, to be polite. Given
reasonable instruction and a proper example, the gifted child
will learn more quickly than an average child. Nevertheless,

the parent who thinks that his child will automatically acquire these desirable traits is expecting far too much.

Parents may also demand higher achievements than their child's abilities warrant because they overestimate his gifts. Some parents think their child is exceptionally bright because he does well in school as a result of normal intelligence combined with diligent application. Such a combination of traits is often more valuable than undisciplined giftedness and may lead to substantial personal success. But it would not be fair to ask such a child, already working at his peak, to do even better.

Other parents, while their children actually are gifted, think they are even more gifted than is actually the case. One such child, finding he could never meet his parent's expectations, no matter how hard he tried, finally gave up and let his schoolwork slip. Upset by this, his parents checked with his teacher and learned they had an exaggerated idea of his capacities. Somewhere along the line they had gotten the impression their youngster qualified as virtually a genius. Actually, he barely qualified as gifted and was simply unable to reach the stratospheric heights of achievement that his parents expected. Parents of children who have been selected for special classes are more likely to err this way than others.

No matter how advanced a child may be intellectually, he is not likely to be equally advanced either emotionally or socially. The six-year-old with an I.Q. of 150 may have the intellectual ability of the average nine-year-old. Yet his feelings and his behavior are probably near the seven-year-old level. Just as he may be big enough to play with seven-year-olds, he feels and acts like these children or, slightly older ones, but not like those whose mental equal he is.

Many parents, however, make the mistake of treating the child as if he were emotionally much older than his years.

To illustrate how a gifted child's mind functions at a more advanced level than his heart, one expert on child behavior reported the story of a boy who was gifted enough to teach himself to read at the age of four. Yet, for his fifth birthday, he asked for three gifts—an atlas, a set of bow and arrows, and a toy he could cuddle.

Some parents try to force-feed talents into a child. They do this without paying attention to whether the child is really gifted in the direction they are trying to push him. One mother, who lived next door to a seven-year-old boy who was an exceptionally talented musician, announced that her child would soon outdo him. Her baby was eleven months old and had not, as yet, given any sign of possible giftedness in music, although he was a bright baby.

The recent prominence on radio and television of children who have succeeded in storing an exceptional number of facts in their heads has made more than one parent commit the error of trying to turn his own child into a replica of these youthful celebrities.

"My father is grooming me for a television-quiz program," a six-year-old reported one day. "He thinks that since I like sports and know a lot about them there is no reason why I shouldn't earn some money toward my college education. Except for one thing," the boy continued sadly, "Now that I have to tell Dad every night what new facts I learned about sports, it isn't fun any more."

Parents who are tempted to try molding their children into entertainers should remember that the children whose knowledge has been displayed before the public learned so much because they were interested in what they were studying, not because they had to learn. Forcing a child to study because of commercial motives will only arouse the child's resentment and resistance.

Studies of children who have become prominent on these programs have shown that their parents devoted a great deal of time to their children's development without thinking of how their knowledge would be used. For example, a study of the home environment of the early Quiz Kids showed that the typical home atmosphere was affectionate. The families were closely knit. The children were neither overindulged nor overprotected. Discipline was firm but kindly. Parents and children shared many activities. In every case the parents gave their children a great quantity of time and attention.

Trying to turn children into quiz contestants is, of course, just a new twist on an old parental error. Many a child has had to spend hated hours facing a piano keyboard or hunched over a violin because his parents decided they, too, would produce a musical prodigy.

Often, the child showed no talent for music. At other times, overeager parents have seized on a child's expression of interest in music and forced him to concentrate on lessons to a far greater extent than he wished or his talents warranted.

Even children with genuine artistic talent have sometimes rebelled when lessons were rammed down their throats. Jessica showed unusual talent for the piano when she was a child and her mother spared no expense in getting her teachers. Mother paid no attention to the fact that Jessica did not want to be a concert artist and practiced only because she preferred to give in to her mother rather than fight with her.

At eighteen, Jessica's musical ability won her a college scholarship. At this point, Jessica rebelled. She told her mother than since she had earned the scholarship, she would use it as she chose. Shortly after, she enrolled at the local university's school of business and from then on refused to play.

Some parents try to achieve their own unfulfilled dreams through their children without concerning themselves as to what might be the children's dreams. The mother who longed to become an actress and therefore forces her little girl to take unwanted dancing, singing, and dramatic lessons is trying to relive her own life through her child rather than help the child develop in her own way. Similarly, many a father has tried to induce his son to go into the family business even though the boy had different interests. Such parents are often not even aware of the unfair pressures they are exerting on their children.

Other parents set vocational goals for their children because they think they detect certain aptitudes in them even though the child is too young to have formed any definite interests of his own. Not long ago a newspaper's advice column carried this letter:

"Our two-year-old son is brilliant and we're very proud of him.

"My husband is an attorney and so is his father. My dad is an engineer. It's natural for a father to want his son to step into his footsteps. But I don't believe this is always best.

"The way our son handles blocks and builds things I know he would be a truly great engineer if encouraged along these lines."

Very sensibly, the columnist pointed out that the child was obviously too young to show any interest in either law or engineering, that it would be a long time before any vocational decision had to be made, and by that time the child would and should make up his own mind.

Some parents, on the other hand, concentrate so hard on doing everything possible for their child that they actually exploit themselves. It is possible to try to do too much even for a highly gifted child. The story has been told of the mother who wanted to make sure her eight-year-old boy had all the time necessary for his intellectual development. She dressed him, bathed him, tended him constantly, and allowed him to do nothing for himself that she could do for him. Her explanation for this suffocating attention was that she wanted him to have all his time free for "creative thinking."

Most self-exploiting parents are not so extreme, but it is possible to do more for a child than is good for either the parents or the child. Many parents write to find out if their children will be eligible for admission to the Hunter School if they move to New York. In almost every case, the family would have to tear up its roots and make a change it could ill afford. These parents explain they want to do "everything possible" for their children. They fail to realize that everything can be too much.

It is true that most communities lack the school programs and other facilities that gifted children could utilize so profitably. It is equally true that special gifts may warrant special training at an early age. But, in most cases, the gifted child is usually better off staying in his home community within the most constructive environment his parents can devise. Later chapters will offer suggestions as to what parents can do to provide their children with varied learning opportunities.

When parents overextend themselves in their efforts to do as much as possible for their child, they actually put heavier pressure than they realize on the child. Being bright and sensitive, the child realizes the extent of the efforts made in his behalf. Since he is the focus of so much family effort and the cause of great financial sacrifice, he feels forced to extend himself and carries a feeling of guilt for the burden he is imposing on his parents. Often parents cannot restrain themselves from expressing their disappointment if the child does not meet their expectations once they have sacrificed so much for him. In the long run, frictions are created between parents and child that outweigh the supposed advantages the parents originally sought.

More important to the gifted child than educational toys, cultural opportunities, special schooling, music lessons, or anything else devoted parents may lavish on the gifted child, is the proper emotional environment. If he lives in a happy household, the gifted child can overcome other inadequacies. Without the tender and loving care that every child requires, no other "advantages" will make up for the lack.

As one educator who is concerned with exceptional children puts it, the gifted child needs to have his parents give him three things. These are acceptance, understanding, and guidance.

The parents of the gifted child must accept him as being a child and as being gifted. He has all the doubts and insecurities of any child. Being gifted, he also has exceptional ability that he must learn to utilize most constructively.

The parent must understand this dual problem. This means realizing that, on one hand, he will react like a child to all the common childhood experiences. Sometimes he will be disobedient, he will get into an occasional scrap with playmates, he will need reassurance after childhood mishaps and mistakes. The familiar statement, "A child needs love most when he is the most unlovable," applies to bright children even more than to others.

At the same time, the fact that he is gifted will require parents to understand that although his mind will range farther and faster than that of the average child, he will still need to be taught how to use this superior mental equipment most effectively. An athlete cannot go far with untrained muscles, but has to train diligently in order to perfect his physical skills. The gifted child must train his mind just as hard as the athlete trains his muscles in order to bring his intellectual skills to their sharpest possible pitch.

This requires the third support that parents have to provide their gifted children—guidance. The intellectually gifted child's need for guidance is like the physically gifted child's need for skilled coaching. The young athlete, however, has an advantage. If he is good at games, automatically he is popular with his fellows. He can improve his skills by playing after school hours. His parents will usually approve of his activities, the school generally has teams that he can join, his classmates look up to him.

If he concentrates seriously on sports and has to keep a training schedule, he gets his rewards every week when he goes out on the gym floor or the ball field and plays with his team while the rest of the school watches and applauds. In addition, he has the opportunity to receive skilled instruction from the team coach. Thus the boy who shows aptitude for basketball, for example, has all the incentives he needs to work at improving himself.

On the other hand, intellectually gifted children are practically on their own. Most schools have no special classes or facilities for the intellectually gifted and so there is no equivalent of the "team" for him to join and thus be able to practice with those who share his skills, his interests, and his level of ability. Sometimes he is lucky and an interested teacher will try to coach him. But unlike the physically gifted, who have special instructors assigned to work with them, there is usually no one who has time officially set aside to train the intellectually gifted. The teacher who tries to give the gifted child extra attention must, as a rule, do it on his own initiative. Time must be taken from other members of the class in order to do so. Under these circumstances, the most interested teacher cannot give much special attention to the gifted child who is in his classroom.

In addition, the development of the gifted mind is even more complex and demanding than the development of the gifted body. As many experts have pointed out, the exceptional mind must be stimulated early and encouraged from childhood on, if it is to reach its full potential growth. The physically superior child develops during his early years largely by playing and letting nature takes its course. Play comes naturally to him. It is part of his everyday life, his success is encouraged by his playmates, and circumstances contribute to motivate him to improve himself.

But the mentally superior child faces a set of obstacles. He cannot easily get the training he needs. He often does not get approval from his classmates for being brighter than they, but in contrast may be spurned by them. Special efforts to give him the individual opportunities he needs to develop his particular skill may be rejected by the child himself because he does not wish to be conspicuous.

Given these circumstances, it is not surprising that many gifted children fail to develop their potential capacities. For many children, it is too easy to become discouraged, too hard to overcome the many obstacles that lie in the way of intellectual self-development.

This is the problem that faces the parent who wants to guide his gifted child to make the fullest use of his abilities. Once the parent recognizes that his child is gifted, he has to help him to develop himself. The parent interested in his child's intellectual development has no alternative but to accept the responsibility of being the youngster's "coach," the one who has to set up his "training schedule," see that he gets his workouts, and pits his mental muscles against steadily increasing challenges so that they do not grow stale from disuse.

To accomplish this difficult task, parents have to help their children acquire two vital characteristics without which giftedness cannot be developed—motivation and discipline. Motivation will make the child want to learn. Discipline, which really means the self-discipline that causes one to stick to a task, will make him capable of learning. If the parent can make these two qualities part of the child's character, he will give him the tools through which he can achieve confident, self-reliant, well-trained maturity.

CHAPTER FIVE

The Job of the Parents

EDUCATORS have a word for the technique of making a child want to learn. They call it "motivating" him. Parents who are interested in inducing their child to make the most of his gifts are concerned with the same problem. They, too, must find ways of motivating him to learn.

The parents of a bright child start with a valuable advantage. A child is naturally curious. The brighter he is, the more things interest him and the more he wants to learn.

As he grows and becomes increasingly aware of the world around him, his questions pour out. He seems to want to know everything. He'll ask why the sky is blue and why he must be the first one in the house to go to bed. Through the answers he is given, and the manner in which he is answered, the child develops his first attitudes toward learning and toward education.

The child does not realize his education has begun. Most of the time, as he explores a new and fascinating world, he just thinks he is having fun. Unfortunately, for most children the feeling that learning is fun rarely lasts very long. For most of them, education becomes something dull and necessary. It is possible, however, for learning to remain an enjoyable activity—even for adults—as *Time* magazine pointed out in an article on this country's leading physicists:

"Asked what he is doing, the scientist is likely to reply, disconcertingly, that he is having 'fun'—a word that occurs again and again, along with 'adventure,' when scientists talk about their work. This sense of joy and excitement that scientists find in their work flatly contradicts the layman's image of science as a gray, austere calling, suited only to eccentrics."

The parents' task is to make learning continue to be fun for the child by making it both enjoyable and rewarding for him to acquire knowledge. Depending on how it is handled, learning can be a game or a chore.

Parents can encourage their child to be interested in learning by showing that they approve of the child's efforts to gain knowledge. Children want their parents' approval. If they find that their parents look on education favorably, that learning brings them parental approval, they will look on the whole educational process as something desirable.

Education starts in the home, therefore, long before the child gets to school. The first attitudes toward learning are taught by the parent long before the child ever meets a school teacher. The parent who dismisses a child's questions with an impatient answer discourages further questioning. The parent who seems pleased to be asked for information encourages his child to seek more knowledge.

In a newspaper interview, the father of a boy whose knowledge of science kept television audiences engrossed for many successive weeks described how he and his wife handled his son's questions:

"He was always curious. We just helped him along, showed him where to find things out for himself, answered his questions when we could.

"Sometimes I would explain something and he would want

to know 'why' and I had to say, 'I just don't know why, let's see where we can find out.'"

Encouraged to be curious and shown how to gather information, this boy kept on learning and rapidly expanded his store of information.

Many parents would like to help their children in the same way, but are afraid to try because they cannot answer many of their children's questions. As one father put it, "I would have to be a whole quiz panel wrapped up in one person to answer all of my five-year-old's questions. Frankly, I'm afraid that if I keep saying I don't know the answers, he'll lose respect for me. So I just say I'm tired or I'm busy, and tell him to go find out for himself."

It is good for a child to look things up for himself. But learning how to look things up is something he has to be taught how to do and he has to be made to feel it is something he should want to do. The best way for a parent to develop this attitude in his child is by making research an activity they share, at least until the child is capable of doing his own research. Instead of saying, "go look it up" and thereby discouraging the youngster from going any further, the parent should say, "let's look it up." When the child finds it is fun to do, he will start looking things up by himself. In the preschool and elementary school years particularly, while the child is actually learning how to learn, parents should participate as much as possible in the child's learning activities.

As parents read about the new discoveries made by scientists who are often still quite young, as they see children demonstrating on television how much information can be stored in a child's mind, they often wonder what it is that starts a person on the intensive search for knowledge. The child diligently picking up and discarding bits of rock as he looks for one particular specimen that he wants for his collection is showing the same kind of persistence as the chemist patiently testing innumerable variations of a formula in order to develop a new product. They are both willing to work hard and patiently to find what they are looking for. The reason is that they are intensely interested in what they are doing and are eager to achieve their goal.

Educators have long stressed that if you want a youngster to learn you have to motivate him. In other words you have to make him *want* to learn. You do this by capturing his interest and making him feel he will accomplish something very much worthwhile.

The sooner a child is motivated to learn and impressed with the desirability and importance of acquiring knowledge, the better are his chances of developing his intellectual gifts to the maximum. Psychologists who have studied at what point famous men began to display and use their gifts stress the value of early motivation to learn. Giving a child this early start is primarily the responsibility of his parents.

There is no special formula for parents to use in stimulating their children's minds. The thing to remember is that the child needs help and encouragement. The exact methods parents use to encourage a child to learn, and exactly what he learns, are of secondary importance. Since radio's Quiz Kids were probably the earliest group of exceptionally informed children to come to widespread popular attention, it might be informative to illustrate how the parents of some of these children stimulated their interest in learning.

One boy, for example, started learning about the world around him while he was still in the high chair. His father would explain to him what the different objects around him, such as plates and spoons, were made of and where they came from. As the child grew older and his curiosity expanded, his parents showed him how to use encyclopedias and other reference books.

When another one of these youngsters was two, he and his

mother started having short bedtime chats about the day's happenings. As he grew older, the subjects of the family discussions became broader and the child was encouraged to start keeping scrapbooks about subjects that interested him. He was not pushed into any particular subject but encouraged to dig deeper into everything that aroused his curiosity.

The exact manner in which parents stimulate their children's interest in learning is not the important point. What should be remembered is that no child learns alone. Every child who manages to acquire a large body of information at an unusually early age has received an exceptional amount of attention and help from someone, usually in the home.

One of the most impressive testimonials to the important role parents play in furthering a child's education and personal development was given by Charles Van Doren, the college instructor who became one of the country's best-know quiz contestants. He demonstrated that a college instructor could not only be a specialist in his own field but have a wide range of general knowledge. He also showed that the gifted can be good humored and personable in addition to being well informed. When Van Doren was asked how he began acquiring so much information in so many fields, he answered that his parents always answered his questions, no matter how insignificant they seemed to be.

Parents should not make the mistake of trying to turn their children into specialists on any particular subject. If learning itself is made interesting, children will develop a variety of interests. A few will find at an early age that one subject interests them particularly, but most children will have many interests and hobbies over the years. The parents' task is not to get a child to pick a vocation before he gets to school, but to get him interested in learning generally.

Thus, the first two steps in getting a child to use and develop his intellectual gifts are:

1. Get him interested in acquiring knowledge.

2. Give him a positive attitude toward the importance of learning.

Once parents have started their child in this direction it is time to give some attention to the third step in developing good learning habits. This is self-discipline.

Self-discipline in learning becomes most important as the gifted child begins to go up through the grades of school. But the groundwork has to be laid in the home early in life.

Nothing new is ever created without first going through failures, revisions, adaptations, and final improvements. The chemist who refuses to give up after the first few failures but patiently mixes his formulas time after time has disciplined himself to continue until he succeeds. Those who are determined to surmount early disappointments can eventually succeed. Those who give up, inevitably fail.

This refusal to give up, despite early failure, is what every child must develop in order to make the most of his gifts. The late Dr. Ernest O. Lawrence, the Nobel prize-winning physicist who invented the atom smasher, put it this way:

"You don't have to have genius to be a scientist—just character. All you have to do is work hard and figure things out."

Training in self-discipline can begin with a child's first independent activities and the first games he plays by himself. Parents should set standards of quality in what the child does, not by making harsh demands but by making a good job part of the game. Putting his toys away when he has finished playing is practically the first step in teaching a child self-discipline.

One child liked to cut figures of people and animals out of magazines and paste them together on cardboard to create story-telling scenes. His mother made it part of the game to cut the figures out neatly, by showing him how much better they looked. A father who takes his child fishing with him put him in charge of the tackle box. Unless everything is in its proper compartment, they can't start out.

Self-discipline includes neatness in handling materials, persistence despite obstacles, patience despite frustration. It means wanting to do something so much that one is ready to put up with difficulties in order to achieve a goal.

This kind of self-discipline is not learned through any one activity. It has to be made part of the child's life by being part of his whole home environment. It develops as he is taught to keep his clothes and his room neat, to put his books away when he is through with them, to accept the fact that he cannot always have what he wants and will often have to wait before his desires are met.

Teaching a child self-discipline does not mean keeping up a constant barrage of corrections and a continuing pressure to achieve. A compliment for something accomplished is more effective than a criticism for some failure. When a child is trying to draw, for example, find something to praise, such as his colors, instead of criticizing the quality of his work. Never volunteer help until he asks for it. Training in neatness and in attention to detail can come from seeing to it that he cleans up properly when finished.

Giving well-deserved praise is one of the best ways of encouraging a child to do his best. This is important because it helps him develop a good opinion of his own capacities and thus provides him with the incentive to live up to his promise. Many gifted children do very ordinary work in school until they are told by a teacher that they are really very bright and could do much better work if they tried. Such children are often surprised. They had not been encouraged to do any better at home. Given a new view of their real abilities, they often concentrate on their work and their grades shoot up.

While it is important for all children to learn to apply themselves diligently, it is especially important for gifted children because learning is so easy for them at first. Since they find during the early school years that they can accomplish as much as is required of them with hardly any effort, they think they will always be able to coast.

Later, when the competition gets stiffer and first-rate achievement requires diligent application to the problem at hand, those who have not learned to apply themselves fall by the wayside. They grow impatient if they don't succeed at the first try and stop trying. This is where the "character" that Dr. Lawrence spoke of comes into play. Those who have it will keep plugging. Such children will probably achieve more than others who may be naturally more gifted than they, but have not learned to discipline themselves.

The most important way the child learns is through the examples set by his parents. All children imitate their parents, and gifted children do so especially, because they are so observant and quick to learn. Parents who want a gifted child to develop good work habits and manners must see to it that they, themselves, do as they tell the child to do. In this respect the parent is much more influential than the teacher because the parent has the child first and sets the patterns of the child's behavior.

The extent to which children imitate their parents was studied at Hunter by observing twenty families who each had three gifted children that attended the school. Although every one of the children differed from the others in his own family, each family threesome had certain traits in common that could be traced back to their parents. For example:

1. *Courtesy.* If one child showed good manners in addressing adults, it was found that the younger two eventually did likewise when they came to the school. The opposite was similarly true, as in one family where the mother always mentioned the teachers' names at home without using Miss or Mrs. When the youngest child's teacher commented to the mother during a visit that her child often did not address her properly in the classroom, the mother said that she had received the same complaint from the teachers of the two

older children and that he must have picked it up from them.

2. *Conscientiousness.* Among the families, some mothers regularly neglected to sign papers, failed to send back report cards on time, forgot to provide their children with work materials, often did not remember to give their children money for lunch or transportation. Invariably their children showed the same kind of carelessness. They forgot their homework, did not bring smocks back to school after taking them home for laundering, and left notes in coat pockets instead of giving them to the teacher, among other things.

3. *Popularity.* While not all the children from the same family were equally popular, they all followed the same general trend. If the first one who came to the school got along well with his classmates, the younger ones who eventually followed also got along—at least fairly well. The reverse was also true. If the first had difficulty making friends, it turned out that the others did not get along too well, either. Each set of children had acquired the social habits of their parents. The parents of the more popular children usually took more active part in the Parents' Association and were often elected to offices. If the children did not get along easily, it turned out that the parents were aloof. If the children showed a tendency to be critical and complaining, it was generally true that their parents were fault-finders.

4. *Generosity.* Parents who were generous in contributing time to the school by volunteering their services, or whose financial contributions were higher than would be expected from persons in their financial circumstances, turned out to have children who were comparably generous. These were the children who frequently offered to help others in class. When they brought treats from home, they made sure they had enough to share with every classmate and not with only a few best friends.

5. *Neatness*. Forms that the school sent home to parents came back either neatly and carefully filled out or obviously done in hasty carelessness. The children's own work showed similar qualities. In some cases it was almost unnecessary to have any names on the papers, for whether exceptionally well done or particularly untidy, it was easy to see that the work belonged to children from the same family. A child who might make an attempt at good penmanship under the influence of a particular teacher eventually reverted to carelessness unless the parents showed their continuing approval of the effort at self-improvement and set good examples themselves.

Many more descriptions could be given of how parents influence their children's work and study habits and thus do much to determine the children's school progress and life achievement. One of the most interesting examples of how the Parents' Association influenced many of the children in the school—and then were influenced by the children—is the case of a theater benefit that the parents sponsored. They bought a block of theater tickets for one night's performance. Money was raised by reselling the tickets at a higher price. There was much arranging and many telephone conversations as to how much money was to go to a charity for children abroad and how much to the school's athletic fund.

Some time after the benefit, a committee of children came to say they wanted to put on their own benefit performance in the school auditorium. As had their parents, they wanted to contribute some of the money for athletic equipment and the rest to a fund for needy children. They got permission, printed tickets by hand, sold them, and the show was put on successfully.

The children's committee came back to discuss what to do with the proceeds. They had decided, they said, to give all of the money to the children's fund and none to their own school. It was explained that while this was a generous gesture, it violated a promise they had made in selling the tickets, when contributors were told they would be giving some of the money for the school's athletic fund.

The children sat in deep thought, wrestling with this conflict between honesty and charity. Finally, one of them saw a solution. "We didn't say how we would divide the contributions," he pointed out. "Let's ask every class to vote on whether they'll give one per cent of the money for bats and balls and ninety-nine per cent for the foreign children." The student vote was overwhelmingly in favor of the proposal. The school got two bats and two balls and a generous check went overseas.

When the parents learned they had been outdone by the children, they first thought of contributing to the athletic fund to compensate for the donation. On second thought, they wisely decided to let the children feel they had made a sacrifice and not destroy the glow that came from doing so.

Just as children are influenced by their parents, they have at the same time a genuine appreciation of the efforts that parents make in their behalf. Gifted children are especially discerning. The material things their parents give them are received appreciatively. But they are most grateful for their parents' time, attention, and personal assistance.

In order to learn what parents do that gifted children especially appreciate, three hundred and fifty Hunter children were asked to respond to the following statements:

"Almost all parents are very kind to their children. They give them food, clothing, a good home, and some money to spend.

"My parents do these things, too, but in addition they do special things that I like. Some of these are below."

Almost all of the children emphasized activities they shared with their parents. Many of them mentioned how much they enjoyed dining out with their parents in different restaurants, particularly those that served foreign food. They liked being taken on trips, especially, as one youngster put it, "to places most children of my age don't get to go to." Many mentioned their pleasure when a companion of their own age also came along.

A great many of the children stated how much they enjoyed the time they could spend with their fathers. The boys often spoke of attending sports events with them or sharing in outdoor activities at an earlier age than is customary. Even a walk was an enjoyable event if it could be shared with a parent. One boy wrote:

"My father and I walk the baby carriage together to give my mother a break, but I am the one who really gets the break for it gives me a chance to talk to Dad uninterrupted."

A girl wrote: "Mother goes places and does things she is not interested in because I like them."

Both the boys and girls were pleased when their fathers let them visit their places of business. A number were excited to get a chance to operate the office machines. Many of the children noted how much they appreciated their parents' participation in such school activities as the Parents' Association and visits to the school that took time from their social activities.

The children generally recognized their parents' thoughtfulness and commented on it. At the same time they often recognized when they, themselves, might be too demanding. One youngster commented:

"If I ask for something I don't always get it, but if it's reasonable, I do."

One of the boys noted gratefully that his father brought home a particular newspaper so that he could read a favorite comic strip, even though his father preferred another paper.

Nothing was appreciated by the children so much as the time busy parents set aside for them. These remarks were typical:

"Mom and Dad sure like us a lot, for they give up their own plans to make Sunday *our* day."

"Busy as she is, my mom is always there if anything happens. She teaches my brother and me the difference between right and wrong."

"Both of my parents are always willing to hear what I have to say at supper unless we have company."

Help with school problems was mentioned many times. One child wrote:

"My father is always ready to put all of the knowledge he has into my head."

As with all children, the gifted want sympathy and understanding and they are grateful when they receive it.

"Mother is comforting when I am sad or moody or have done something wrong."

"Dad always talks to me as if I am a grownup, which I love."

"Mother helps with my problems and is interested in the things I do. She discusses matters with me."

"Mother is very nice to come to when you're feeling blue. She is very calm and doesn't get excited when I do."

"Dad never raises his voice. He drives a fair bargain with me."

At the same time that the children expressed their gratitude for what their parents do for them, many showed the insight that gifted youngsters often possess.

"Mother and Father help me by quarreling only when they think I am asleep, although usually I am not. Nevertheless, I appreciate their effort."

"Both of my parents are very kind to me. When they are a unit together, they are better than ever."

In describing the traits the children especially liked in their parents, these terms appeared most often:

Understanding, Humorous (has a sense of humor), Sympathetic, Good Cook (they liked having their favorite foods prepared for them), Kind, Loving, Patient.

The way children can be impressed so that they wish to follow a parent's example was expressed by one little girl who said:

"My mother is beautiful like a flower in bloom. She is so neat and clean I want to be like her."

It is interesting to note that it was the efforts made by their parents to share activities with them that the children appreciated most. Surprisingly, not one child mentioned parties planned for them as something they especially appreciated. Some of the children were questioned personally about this omission. Yes, many said, they always had parties given for them on their birthdays. But, so far as the children were concerned, a birthday party did not compare in importance to a long, friendly walk in the park, a chance to use Dad's workshop tools, or some help from Mother in baking a cake. One little girl summed up the children's attitude toward parties with these words:

"When you've been to one, you've been to all. Even when your mother tries to be original, she doesn't change things much except the table decorations. Sometimes it's fun if you get to plan them, but usually they want to surprise you."

Music lessons and summer camps were similarly ignored by most of the children. They were more accepted than enjoyed, so far as most of the children were concerned.

The majority of the children wanted more independence. By the time they are seven, many are already pleading for a chance to use public transportation by themselves and to go alone to school.

As these responses show, even at a comparatively early age children are already aware of, and responsive to, the example and influence of their parents. One of the best illustrations of the importance of a home environment that produces strong motivation to achieve is shown in Professor Terman's study of gifted children. Eighteen years after the study began, Professor Terman made a special study of his gifted subjects to learn how they had been doing in the world. Six hundred of the men were classified in A, B, and C groups, depending on how much of a "success" they appeared to be making of their lives. They were not rated on how much money they were earning, but on how constructively they had been using their superior intellectual ability.

When the A's and C's, about a hundred and fifty of each, started out in elementary school they were about the same in intelligence and in their school grades. In high school the C's began to show lower marks. The big slump came with college. Of those whose success rating put them in the A group, 90% graduated from college. Among the C's less than half were college graduates. Of those in the two groups who were graduated from college, the A's scored markedly higher in their grades. At the same time, twice as many A's as C's participated in extracurricular activities. More A's married and fewer of them divorced. Even though earnings were not the basis of their success rating, the A's averaged substantially higher incomes than the C's.

Looking back into the life histories of those who made up the two groups, Terman found that the most important difference was in the type of family they came from. The families from which the A's came turned out to be more stable, better adjusted, and much more concerned with education. So far as the A's and C's themselves were concerned, Terman found that they differed in two ways. The A's were emotionally better adjusted and they had a greater drive to achieve.

High motivation to achieve is not something that is set and finally accomplished at any one stage in the child's life. It is something that begins in the period before he starts school, develops in the early school years, and is usually finally cemented early in high school. If a child is encouraged to learn early in life and he is given opportunities and incentives to achieve as he grows older, his motivation will strengthen and help carry him upward to worthwhile achievement in high school, college, and later. If the child is not fortunate enough to be given continuing incentives to utilize his capacities, he is likely to stop making the efforts necessary for continued success.

At the same time that parents are encouraging their child to make the best possibe use of his intellectual gifts, they should keep an eye on whether he is developing other aspects of his personality. The body has to grow as well as the mind and it is sometimes necessary to assist a child in developing his physical along with his mental skills.

Social skills, too, have to be learned. Getting along with playmates is preparation for getting along at school and later for being able to work effectively with fellow employees. Important as it is to develop ideas, one should then be able to communicate them and convince others to try them. Even when personableness is not necessary for professional success, life is pleasanter if one has the ability to handle oneself with ease in the world at large.

Just as parents guide a child's eating habits so that he has a well-balanced diet, they should similarly guide his use of his time so that his activities are well balanced. The child who reads constantly is like the child who eats too much of one food. Even a good thing can be overdone. This does not mean that parents should snatch away a book that their child is interested in and force him out to play. If a book or some activity has him absorbed at the moment, his interest in the outdoors will not be aroused by forcing him to join in a baseball game.

One of the reasons children sometimes fail to develop ease in getting along with others is that their time is overplanned. There is such a thing as too many lessons and too many planned activities. So far as learning opportunities are concerned, a child can be overenriched as well as undernourished. A child needs time when he is free of obligations and can do what he wants, even if he wants to do nothing. Everyone needs time to sit quietly in a corner with his own thoughts.

One child noted that he had a "Meditation Spot" and no one in the house disturbed him when he sat there. "It's a great relief," he added.

The same principles of encouragement and providing opportunities may have to be used for a child who is shy or is not good at games as were used to motivate him to explore intellectual interests. Since the gifted child is further advanced intellectually than he is in his physical growth, he may sometimes become discouraged by his seeming lack of skill when he tries to play. At this point, a boy may need father's encouragement and help. If the two of them have a few private practice sessions, the child will get a chance to improve his skills and be encouraged to go out and play with children of his own age.

But just as a child should not be forced into some hobby or vocational interest "for his own good," he should not have to play a game he does not like. Not everybody enjoys playing football or any other particular game and the gifted child is entitled to choose his play activities as well as his books and hobbies. Tennis, for example, calls for as much speed, precision, and timing as basketball. A child may actually be showing good judgment in preferring tennis, since it is a game he can continue to play as an adult. Similarly, if a boy has no appetite for baseball, his father may find that teaching him to play golf gives him an opportunity to share an activity with his son and also gets the boy outdoors. More and more boys are bowling with their fathers when outdoor sports are not possible.

Another aspect of the same problem may show up when

the gifted child tries to work with his hands. No matter how well-developed he may be for his age, he almost always sets a higher standard for himself than he can reach and, therefore, is disappointed with the results. This applies equally to a girl trying to sew and a boy trying to saw.

Because a gifted child often learns to write at an early age, his penmanship may be poor. He cannot control his pencil well enough to write clearly. Also, he may be in such a hurry to get his ideas down that he finds himself held back by having to handle the "tools" of writing and gets impatient. Later he may want to build something with his father's tools but may be clumsy in handling them. Such failures can discourage a child from further efforts unless his parents help and encourage him. While he is still quite young they should expect that his physical co-ordination may not be any better than that of average youngsters his age. If he still needs help as he gets older, they should work with him as they would in helping him with sports and other activities.

The parents' problem in raising a gifted child can be summed up by these questions: How can I enable my child to develop as fully as possible those abilities in which he is superior to others at the same time that I help him realize his own limitations? How can I help him to get along in the everyday world as a well-balanced individual?

To meet this requirement a parent has to help his child develop into a person who is studious yet sociable, self-confident but modest, independent without becoming eccentric, persistent in pursuing his own interests but patient with the lesser capacities of others and respectful of their efforts.

As can be seen, this means helping the gifted child to attain an objective attitude toward himself and toward life in general. The best start toward attaining these goals comes through the guidance and example set by parents.

This means teaching the gifted child both respect for

others and helping him acquire the strength of character to be himself and not bow to the unreasonable demands of others. It means teaching him the dignity of independence and the danger of overconformity.

In addition, attaining a balanced outlook on life means not overemphasizing intellectual attainments so that they become a means of showing off. One little girl had her achievements made so much of at home that she could not bear to be caught in an error in school. If her teacher pointed out a mistake she secretly tried to correct it before taking her paper home.

Parents may contribute to the child's feeling that perfection in itself is more important than the manner in which it is achieved by doing the child's homework for him, so that he can get a perfect grade from the teacher. The child may, at first, feel guilty as he receives the teacher's praise for work he has not done, but he soon learns to accept such a procedure when he finds his parents approve of it.

At the same time, helping a child attain a sense of balance should not mean encouraging him to hide his gifts in order to be "popular," as did one teen-age girl. She carefully made a certain number of errors on her exams so that she would not achieve a higher mark than most of the boys.

To guide the child between these two rows of pitfalls and in a straight line toward the attainment of maximum personal achievement and satisfaction is a job that requires time and effort. Parents should not feel guilty if they sometimes do not feel up to making these extra efforts. No parent has either the time or the patience to act constantly as an imaginative instructor and companion. The most devoted of parents can run out of patience when the questions get out of hand. Many parents often feel like the weary mother who admitted, "sometimes I wish my children would just do what I tell them without asking for detailed explanations."

A parent should unashamedly admit to himself that he is

sometimes too tired or too out of sorts to cope with the demands of a gifted child. Instead of feeling guilty or neglectful, simply tell the child to question you again at a later time. Or, if it is an activity that you lack the energy to explain or share, make a mental note and simply wait until another opportunity arrives when you feel up to the effort.

No child's life is molded by a single parental action. It is the over-all environment you provide for him that is important. Do not worry about what you may consider an occasional inadequacy as a parent. Encourage yourself by recalling the good things you are doing and the worthwhile results you are getting.

After all, parents are human. They, too, need to be motivated to continue their efforts and, most often, they have to motivate themselves. Parents will need to encourage each other, for no one knows as well as his mother how exasperating a voluble, gifted child can be, except his father.

Check List: Are You a Gifted Parent?

The more gifted a child, the more he needs parents who are gifted in helping him discover and develop his abilities. In that sense the gifted child needs gifted parents.

This check list is not all inclusive and there is no passing score. It is intended as a set of reminders as to what are the most important principles for promoting a child's giftedness. The parent who can answer "yes" to a large proportion of these questions can feel he is effectively promoting his child's gifts.

1. Do you answer your child's questions with patience and good humor?

2. Do you take advantage of his questions and expressions

of interest to guide him into further learning and exploration?

3. Do you help your child develop physical and social skills as carefully as you encourage mental growth?

4. Do you help him learn how to get along with children of all levels of intelligence?

5. Do you avoid criticizing him by comparing him with his brothers and sisters or his companions?

6. Do you set reasonable standards of behavior for your child and then see that he meets them?

7. Do you impose firm and fair discipline that is consistent and neither too harsh nor too permissive?

8. Do you show your child that he is loved for his own sake and not for his intellectual achievements?

9. Do you try to find something specific to praise when he shows you his work? (A generalized compliment means little to gifted children.)

10. Do you help him to select worth-while reading materials and television programs?

11. Do you provide your child with hobby materials and books of his own?

12. Do you provide places where your child can study, work at his hobbies, and display his work?

13. Do you participate in some of your child's activities?

14. Do you let him learn about and share in some of your hobbies and interests?

15. Do you take your child on trips to points of interest?

16. Do you enable your child to take advantage of lessons and activities offered by private groups or community organizations?

17. Do you teach your child how to budget his time, organize his work, and improve his study habits?

18. Do you help your child to make his own plans and decisions?

19. Do you give your child increasing independence as his ability to handle responsibility increases?

20. Do you give him household responsibilities and other tasks suitable for his age?

21. Do you avoid overstressing intellectual achievement?

22. Do you avoid "pushing" your child too hard by not being too demanding about afterschool lessons or activities?

23. Do you resist the impulse to show your child off before relatives and friends?

24. Do you resist any temptation to exploit his gifts commercially?

25. Do you teach him to use his gifts for the benefit of society rather than only for his own selfish purposes?

26. Do you encourage him to set high educational and vocational goals?

27. Do you refrain from trying to pick his vocation for him but try to help him learn about as many occupations as possible?

28. Do your expressions of attitude and your behavior set the example you want your child to follow?

29. Do you avoid talking down to him and speak to him as you do to adults?

30. Do you try to speak as correctly as you want him to do?

Part III

WORKING WITH THE GIFTED CHILD

CHAPTER SIX

The Years Before School

EVERY CHILD needs love, encouragement, opportunity, and discipline. Given these, the average child will go far in developing his inborn capacity. Without them, the most gifted child is likely to flounder.

It is not necessary to know a child's I.Q. in order to help him use it. Whether the child's score is 100, 125, or 150 the same principles apply in order to help him develop his gifts.

If a child turns out to be more gifted, he will probably progress faster, but applying these principles is likely to improve every child's intellectual progress. Most of the children who appear on quiz programs, for example, are not intellectual prodigies. They are usually children of superior intelligence who have benefited from the efforts of exceptionally attentive parents. All over the country other children are receiving similar benefits and have comparable information. In the long run they may be better off by not coming to popular notice at an early age. They are spared pressures that are almost unavoidable when one stands in the limelight.

Although each child is an individual with his own rate of development and his own special characteristics, parents who want to give their youngster the best possible start can proceed on the assumption that the earlier a child is encouraged to use his abilities the better his chances of making the fullest use of them. This does not mean that he will necessarily decide on his field of work while he is still quite young. He may or he may not. But he will have a chance to start developing at an early age the mental skills he will eventually have to apply to any field that interests him and he will have more time to explore various interests.

Since an early start is advantageous in developing a child's intellectual gifts, at what point should parents begin?

Talking: Practically the first thing a baby learns from his parents is how to talk. He learns to speak in the language used in his home. The way he pronounces his words and the size of his vocabulary are influenced by how his parents speak to him.

Parents who use baby talk are hindering their children by teaching them words they will have to unlearn. Words like "moo-moo" and "choo-choo" will have to be discarded after a short time. Why not say "cow" and "train" in the first place?

The same thing applies to parts of the body and bodily functions. Parents and children usually develop private words for these things that eventually have to be unlearned and may create embarrassment if a child grows older without having outgrown them.

One five-year-old, for example, was being tested by a school psychologist who had asked her to draw whatever she liked. In the middle of this effort she looked up and said, "I would like to make a stream." The psychologist told her to go right ahead. What followed had nothing to do with drawing.

The importance of teaching children the right word and the right way to pronounce it from an early age is not so much to avoid this kind of accident as to get the whole process of learning off on the right foot at the very start. As was emphasized earlier, this does not mean that a baby should be given vocabulary drill. He might learn a few additional words that way, but he may develop a distaste for such instruction at the same time. For the preschool child, learning should be a natural part of daily living, not something he does during special practice periods.

Parents might keep these general rules in mind when talking to their children:

1. Don't talk to him in baby talk and don't use babyish enunciation. Always speak distinctly and in an adult manner.

2. When the baby tries to say something, listen patiently and repeat carefully for him the words he needs.

3. Since a child cannot enunciate as clearly as an adult, don't correct him constantly. Speak the same words slowly and correctly when you answer him and he will gradually learn by imitating you.

4. Instead of fussing over his speech, praise him in simple phrases when he does well.

5. Help him to expand his vocabulary by telling him the proper word for objects that interest him. When he sees something and points to it, tell him what it is.

Nursery School: If they think their preschool child is gifted, many parents who are eager "to do the best for my child" try to get the child into a school as quickly as possible. Since the public schools will not accept a child into kindergarten until he is at least five years old, such parents often feel that nursery school is the best way to promote their gifted youngster's development.

Many a three-year-old, therefore, suddenly finds himself in a classroom filled with small strangers while mother waves good-by from outside the door and smiles encouragement. For some children the new experience is something they enjoy. For others, it is an unhappy time, at least until they manage to accustom themselves to their new surroundings.

The question of whether to send a child to nursery school is one of those blamed-if-you-do and blamed-if-you-don't dilemmas that so often afflict the conscientious parent. If they send a child to nursery school, parents ask, are they giving him extra advantages or denying him the benefits he might derive by staying at home? Which is more important, they wonder, professionally supervised group activity or mother's personalized individual attention? How can one tell if a child is ready for nursery school?

Here are some considerations to keep in mind when deciding whether or not to send a child to nursery school:

1. Is the child emotionally ready for nursery school?

At the age of three, nursery-school age, many children are still not ready to adapt themselves to the comparatively impersonal group living that must be part of going to school. Other children, socially more mature, are eager to move into the larger world that nursery school represents. Readiness for nursery school, like readiness for any other learning activity, is a question of individual development that has nothing to do with how gifted the child may be.

Some children still cling to their mother at this age and there is little point in tearing them away from her comfort and protection if it can be avoided. In such cases a child's emotional needs may be fulfilled in a much more satisfactory way by keeping him at home.

A child's readiness to move away from the shelter of his parent can be judged by how independently he plays. If he has a chance to attend nursery school but does not seem interested, if he still stays very close to home whenever he can, he obviously is better off not going to nursery school.

2. Does he prefer to play by himself and in small groups, or does he have many friends?

Parents sometimes decide that their three-year-old should be sent to nursery school so that he will have a large group of playmates. Some parents worry about social maladjustment when they find their child spending part of his time playing all alone. Nursery school, they believe, will teach him to be more sociable.

Actually, at this age most children do not want many friends and a certain amount of aloofness is normal. Often they prefer to play in small groups, with one to three companions. They may also prefer to play alone a good part of the time.

If a child has no playmates of his own age, or if they are all going off to school themselves, nursery school may help him find companions. Similarly, if he plays in large groups he may be showing that he is ready for the comparable environment he will find in the classroom. But if he happily spends a good part of his time with just a few friends and likes to be alone at other times, he is showing normal behavior for his age and parents need not worry.

3. Does the child get a reasonable amount of personal attention at home?

Many parents feel that a child, especially if he is gifted, will have more opportunities for development at nursery school. This may or may not be true. Parents often overlook the fact that if a child is part of a large group he will probably get less personal attention than he might at home.

The teacher whose attention is absorbed by many children cannot give as much time to one youngster's questions as a mother would be able to. On the other hand, a mother busy with a new baby, or with her time taken by other pressing duties, may be so occupied that her child would get more attention at school. Whether a child can get more time given to his individual needs for exercise, play, and rest at home or in nursery school similarly depends on the school's facilities and the mother's schedule. Which turns out to be preferable depends on individual circumstances.

Thus, the decision as to whether or not to send a child to nursery school depends on the child's own expressed desires, his degree of dependency on his mother, his preference for individual or group play, the availability of playmates, the quality of the nursery school's facilities, and the amount of attention he can receive at home.

Parents should also keep in mind that sending a child to both nursery school and kindergarten often means duplicating practically the same activities for two or more years. A bright child, in particular, may grow bored and impatient if he finds himself with the same toys and games for so long and nothing new to challenge his interests. A year of kindergarten is very worth while, but more than that amount of time spent doing the same things is seldom advisable for the gifted child.

Reading: Parents interested in developing their children's gifts probably worry more about reading than anything else. They ask anxiously, should we teach him to read or not? They inquire about a bright four-year-old happily immersed in a picture book, "If my child were really gifted wouldn't he be reading by now?"

A preschool child's interests and learning habits can be developed in many ways. Many parents make the mistake of thinking books are the only tool for developing the preschool child's giftedness. They often concentrate, therefore, on urging the child to read, and neglect the numerous other activities to which a child can be introduced and, through many of these activities, actually encouraged to read.

The preschool child needs his parents more than he needs books. It is they who are his first teachers, encourage him, set standards of achievement, express approval of his accomplishments, and provide continuing opportunities for him to explore new interests. Specific activities through which this can be done will be suggested in the next chapter.

Readiness to read is a very individual thing, even among the gifted. Many gifted children are interested in reading even before they start school, but few of them actually become accomplished readers on their own and many do not begin to read until they are in first grade. After both groups have been in school for a while, it will be impossible to tell who learned in advance and who waited for the classroom.

Parents who wait breathlessly for their child to express an interest in reading, so that they will have proof he is gifted, should keep in mind that early reading is only one of the possible signs of giftedness. If, however, a child does express a desire to read, the same principles that were applied to helping him learn to talk should be used in helping him learn to read.

First of all, make learning to read a natural thing rather than a special activity. Let the child set the pace.

Usually, bright children become interested in reading by inquiring about, and then learning to recognize, individual words that they encounter in their everyday lives. If the child's name is printed on one of his belongings, for example, he may learn to recognize it. The words on his cereal box may come next. If he goes shopping with his mother, he may get interested in grocery signs. More than one child has picked up some of his first words from the block letters announcing the day's specials in the supermarket.

Many children get their early reading lessons from the television set by learning to recognize the names of products. The combination of hearing the word and seeing it, make a strong impression. As one little girl complained, "I have to stop myself when I write some words. Often I write duz instead of does. I wish they wouldn't do things like that to children learning to spell."

Parents should keep in mind that reading is not necessarily learned from books. Labels, posters, signs, newspaper headlines have all served as primers. Whatever printed matter a child gets interested in reading can help him learn to read. One child listened to the Sunday comics being read over the radio and began following them in his own paper. The time for a more selective choice of reading material will come later in the child's reading career.

Writing: Attempts to write usually begin the same way as the first efforts to read. The child may see his name and try to copy it. Or, he copies other words that become familiar. Since coloring and drawing are activities that most children enjoy, writing usually comes naturally as a result. If he wants to write, get a penmanship book entitled *Manuscript Writing.* Let the child copy the letter forms used in this book. Do not let him start with joined letters.

His new interest in writing should not become an excuse for word drill or penmanship lessons. Keep in mind that his muscular co-ordination is probably still not good enough to enable him to write well. Until a teacher gives him formal instruction, he will be best off scribbling on large sheets of paper or on a blackboard.

As much as possible, learning should be a normal part of the day's activities for the preschool child. For example, a child does not learn to talk during a special hour set aside for that purpose. He picks up words as he goes along. In other ways, too, learning should be made as much as possible a normal part of growing.

Emotional Development: The child's emotional development proceeds the same way. Mother does not set aside a specific hour for loving her baby. Sometimes, of course, she is too busy to express her affection, but the child develops the feeling of being loved through all the contacts he has with his parents.

Fathers, especially, should realize that they cannot establish healthy emotional relationships with their children by being a pal once a week and neglecting them for business all the rest of the time. It is difficult for the hard-working father to take time out frequently to concentrate on his child's needs. But whenever he is spending time with his youngster he should keep in mind the importance of contributing to the child's development. The previous chapter has already pointed out how eager children are for their parents' attention and how highly they value the time devoted to them.

Because fathers cannot spend as much time with their children as do mothers, parents often make the error of dividing up certain responsibilities. A common example of this occurs when mothers say to their misbehaving children, "Wait till Daddy comes home. Then you'll get it."

Kisses should not come from one parent and spankings from the other. Affection and discipline should come equally from both parents, psychologists emphasize. Studies have shown also that children have the best chance for healthy development when both parents have equal importance in the household, without either being dominant. It is in such homes, where mother and father have equal status, that children most often grow up to be well-adjusted in their relationships with others.

One reason it is important for fathers to take part in their children's activities is for the value of the example set for the children. Sons who never see their fathers read a book, for example, may get the idea that books are only for sissies. As in most phases of the parent-child relationship, the best teaching is by example.

Selecting Playthings: Unless a preschool program gives a gifted child a chance for personal growth and the enlargement of his interests, he is often better off on his own under the attentive guidance of a parent. Rather than have books and toys assigned to him on the basis of what is considered suited for children his age, he will probably be happier making his own choices.

A gifted child often ignores the toys designed for his particular age group and selects some intended for those older as well as others designed for children who are younger. A gifted five-year-old, for example, might select a comparatively advanced construction set and a big, cuddly teddy bear. His superior imagination enables him to visualize what he can build with the construction set and also enables him to imagine the cuddle toy as perhaps a make-believe brother, sister, or pet.

Because he is in certain ways mature for his age, the gifted child is often given a live pet before he is old enough to care for it. Those who present him with the responsibility for the care of a live animal forget that, in some aspects of maturity, the gifted child is not much more advanced than any child of his age. Expecting a preschool child to accept the advanced responsibility of caring for a pet by himself is often too demanding.

Another way in which the preschool child is often expected to show more advanced development than he has yet achieved is in activities requiring muscular co-ordination. One mother, noting her gifted child's difficulty with art activities in his first grade class, commented worriedly: "I'm afraid my child will never get promoted to second grade. Every time he sees a crayon he starts to cry."

Instructions to be sure to color only "inside the lines" or emphasis on rigid copying may not only be beyond the child's present muscular co-ordination, which prevents him from guiding his crayon or pencil with perfect care, but may inhibit his efforts to use his imagination and be creative.

Experts in children's art instruction agree that it is difficult to pick out the child with genuine artistic talent. Given the opportunity, almost all children enjoy the chance to express themselves by drawing and coloring. The more artistically gifted a child happens to be, the more individuality his work will show. Allowing a child freedom of artistic expression, whether or not he turns out to have special talent, gives him a better chance to develop whatever artistic abilities he may have.

Instead of emphasizing neatness or imitation, therefore, parents should give their child simple materials for drawing and coloring, and step aside. What he draws and what colors he uses are far less important than the chance to explore an interest and express himself. Many children enjoy "painting" with clear water on a wall. They enjoy making brush strokes and find the wet splotches as exciting as using color. Finger painting is another example of the pleasure most children get just from applying some liquid material to a solid surface and creating designs. If a child's interest in art should become serious as he gets older, there will be plenty of time for formal art instruction.

The preschool child usually moves from one interest to the next as each attracts his attention. Parents may make the error of taking a young child's passing expression of interest in any one subject more seriously than it deserves. They may invest in comparatively expensive equipment and materials only to find the child giving up this interest shortly afterward. The microscope he asked for so eagerly may be abandoned a few days after he gets it. Parents who try to coerce the child back to the abandoned activity seldom succeed.

Preschool children's interests are usually short lived. Lasting absorption in an activity, so that it genuinely can be considered a hobby, is not often seen in children of this age. Parents will therefore spare themselves disappointment and expense if they keep this fact in mind and make their purchases accordingly.

Unless the child shows unusually persistent interest in a particular direction, a preschooler's interests almost always can be satisfied with fairly inexpensive materials. Since such materials allow the child to use his imagination, he will probably have even more fun with them than with many expensive toys. A puppet with a head made out of a sponge rubber ball, buttons for eyes, and home-stitched cloth for the body will, in most cases, be more acceptable to the preschooler than an elaborate model purchased in the store.

Many comparably simple materials can be used to develop the preschooler's interests and provide him with activities. The next chapter will offer examples and suggestions.

CHAPTER SEVEN

Working and Playing with the Preschool Child

MOST CHILDREN start out possessing curiosity and imagination. The parent's task is to encourage the continued development of these traits, strengthen the child's interest in learning, and promote the development of good learning habits. Some of the games and activities through which this can be done are outlined on the following pages. Using these suggestions as a start, parents can devise many other activities on the basis of their own and their child's interests and inventiveness.

"Tell me a story," almost every child begs, practically from the time he can speak the sentence. Here is a wonderful chance to start the child on the right intellectual road. Storytelling is an activity that usually is enjoyed by fathers. While mothers should not necessarily be excluded, making this father's special activity gives him an opportunity to share an important experience with his child.

As the stories are read to a child, he develops an appreciation of the books from which they come. He learns to think of books as something exciting. His vocabulary expands and so does his imagination.

There are many lists of recommended books for children of different ages. Every public library offers books for children of different ages and assistance in selecting them, but do not limit yourself to these. Gifted children should not be restricted to books selected for children of lesser ability.

Never hesitate to try a book that seems a bit advanced. Often you will be surprised by the ease with which the child absorbs the material you thought might be too difficult. The famous Dutch author, Hendrik Willem Van Loon, once confided that he always put some long and unusual words into his writings for children. The children loved to learn the strange new words. If it should turn out that a book is too advanced for the child, simply save it for a later time and try another one.

Besides the stories that are read to them, children love to have stories made up especially for them. They need not be very original to absorb the attention of a child. One father made up stories about the daily adventures of a little girl—very like his own, of course—and let her fill in episodes. After a while, they were making up a story together.

As children get a bit more advanced they love to hear true (or at least partly true) stories based on their parents' experiences as children. The children call these reminiscences "Long Ago" or "Old Time" stories, which may startle parents who know the incidents took place not so very long ago. In this way, children begin to get an understanding of time, and the changes it produces, and they develop an appreciation of the modern facilities and comforts with which they have been provided.

A child's interest in words and reading can thus be stimulated in different ways long before he is ready for reading. Some children memorize a large collection of children's poems just by having them read aloud. The mother of one four-year-old played rhyming games with the child. As the mother went about a household task she would make up a sentence describing it, and the child would finish the verse by inventing a rhyme to complete the phrase.

"First we wash each breakfast dish"—her mother began, for example. After a little pondering Carol replied with:

"To make it clean as you can wish."

Not great poetry but quite good for a child, and excellent as a way to get her interested in how words can be used effectively.

Many children become intrigued by words of similar sound. They "collect" them and thus enlarge their vocabularies. One little girl happily reported her discovery that, "When you eat, you say, 'I ate' and there's also the number eight when you count." Children will similarly get interested in words with similar roots like "microphone" and "telephone" and try to see how many such they can discover.

One mother and her little girl played a game in which a category was selected, such as the names of states, countries, birds, or flowers. They then took turns offering names that fitted into the selected category. When they ran out of words, the mother would look up additional ones, which gave the child a chance to acquire new knowledge.

The specific games or activities are not important for themselves. Parents and children will invent different ones that grow out of their own personalities. What is worth remembering is that the time parents and child spend together can be used profitably, and made equally enjoyable for both, if it is turned into a period of learning through playing.

For example, a mother must spend a great deal of time in the kitchen. She can keep her child nearby and occupied during rainy periods, for example, by permitting her bread board to be used as an easel, propping it up against the back of a chair. Or, she might provide a blackboard that stands on a tripod and can be moved back and forth to the child's room. With some colored chalks and an eraser he is all set for drawing and lettering.

When one mother found her child trying to pick out the words on the labels of canned foods, she began stripping the labels for him as she used up the cans. They were pinned up on bulletin boards in the kitchen and the child could study them to his heart's content. If storage space permits, save some of the cans themselves for play materials.

Another mother kept her slightly older child interested and out of mischief by explaining what she was doing while she measured out ingredients. Using doll-sized utensils, the little girl imitated her mother's example in mixing a cake, using "make-believe" ingredients, mainly flour and water. As soon as the youngster was able to do so, mother let her help by holding something. When Sue was old enough to really do her own measuring, she often imitated her mother with ingredients she was given for her own use. She would make her own little salad, for example, or a meat patty, which her mother then cooked for her.

After a while, Sue began cutting advertisements featuring food pictures from the newspaper and magazines and began making a scrapbook. Other children clip pictures that represent different immediate interests. With a stack of old magazines, a blank notebook, plastic scissors, paste or cellophane tape, many children have gained knowledge and pleasure.

Scrapbook materials are all around these days. The daily newspapers, Sunday supplements, and the picture magazines are all good sources. The older child will find much to interest him in seed catalogs, travel folders, and the pictures and advertisements in travel magazines. If you have access to some of the weekly and monthly business magazines, the pictures of vehicles, machinery, and of men doing specialized industrial tasks can open a new world for the youngster who cannot actually see them in action. In this way, the successive exploration of fresh interests becomes part of a child's life.

Parents should not set up an activity and push a child into

it, but make the activity something that he takes to eagerly. The parent can offer a suggestion—"Since you like animals why don't you make an animal dictionary?" The child may take up the idea or not. If he doesn't, something else will come up. Even if he does pursue a particular suggestion, he will undoubtedly drop the project eventually.

This should not concern the parent. The idea is not to have the child complete a given number of projects, but simply to encourage him to explore ideas that interest him. As his interests change, he will be acquiring new knowledge and a constantly broadening sense of the world around him.

In the early years, simple and inexpensive play materials are often the most effective. Brown wrapping paper or paper bags neatly cut open are as satisfying to a child as canvas to an artist. Crayons, powdered paints, and colored pencils are inexpensive and come in enough different colors to give him all the variety he wants. Scraps of cloth and fur, tinsel from the Christmas wrappings, colored paper, the cardboards from father's shirts are all useful. The scraps can be worked into figures as they are pasted on the cardboard, or just combined into a blend of textures and colors in the same way as adult artists create "collages."

Other materials that can be collected in a "treasure box" set aside for the purpose are beads, empty thread spools, buttons, sheets of cellophane, colored netting, corrugated board, stickers, doilies, wool yarn, paper cups, pieces of wooden doweling. There is no telling what the youthful artist or engineer may choose to create from these and similar materials.

One of the best "finger paints" is chocolate pudding. With this material, there's nothing to fear if the youthful artist sucks one of his fingers while waiting for inspiration. On a hot afternoon a child can be put in the tub with pudding paint. When the session is over, the artist and the artwork can be washed off at the same time.

Modeling clay allows a child to dig his hands into his material and mold shapes to his heart's content. Even better—and cleaner—than commercial clay is a mixture of flour and water, with enough salt added to give it the right consistency. Later, when the child has more manual dexterity, he may want to try soap carving. For all such activities, one of father's old shirts with the sleeves cut short make a fine artist's smock.

Many gifted children are fond of jigsaw puzzles. Sometimes a child can put them together so fast that he turns them over and works on the blank side to make it harder. Instead of constantly buying new puzzles for young fans, some ingenious parents make their own. Pictures from magazines, pasted on thin wood or cardboard and cut into irregular pieces, often interest a child more than purchased puzzles.

The advantage of giving the child simple materials is not only that they are inexpensive, but that they help him develop his imagination. One father used to play "Let's Make a Toy" with his two children. When the boy was quite young, a milk carton was given cardboard wheels fastened on with paper fasteners, a piece of string was attached, and it became a wagon to be pulled. For the girl, a section was cut out of an oatmeal container and it became a doll's cradle. In a later, more elaborate version of the boy's toy, a cardboard seat was fastened on for the wagon driver, and the driver, himself, was made of pipe cleaners. For the girl, blankets and a spread made of cloth or paper were added to the cradle. As the children grew older, the toys grew more complicated. Eventually the boy graduated to using his father's power tools and the girl began working on her mother's sewing machine.

Many activities are enjoyed by both boys and girls. Some activities that are thought of as being enjoyed by one sex are often enjoyed by the other also. Little girls, for example, often like to play with toy dishes, serving make-believe meals. If a boy seems to like what goes on in the kitchen, there is no reason to discourage him from learning something about how food is prepared. The enjoyment men show when they preside over a barbecue is evidence that cooking is not solely a feminine interest.

Many lifetime hobbies and vocations have grown out of the pursuit of early childhood interests. An interest in science, for example, can develop from something as simple as a set of mineral specimens. An inexpensive "scientific instrument" that many youngsters enjoy using is a long-handled magnifying glass. With one of these, the inner structure of a flower and the veining of a rock take on a new appearance and increased interest.

A subject that seems to interest many gifted children at a fairly early age is dinosaurs. Their size, strange shapes, and the fact that they are extinct fascinates many children. Seeing pictures of dinosaurs, handling small models of them, and possibly viewing their fossils in a museum has often served as the first peek many a gifted child has taken into the vastness and diversity of nature. Often it has served as an introduction to science.

One boy developed his interest in biology through the ingenious way his father answered his questions about the workings of the human body. Steven's father showed him how mechanical devices were often an imitation of human organs. The camera was an eye, the telephone an ear, and many details of different machines were first found in natural objects. Not an exact comparison, of course, but intriguing enough to get this youngster interested in exploring further how both machines and man work.

Possibly the most effective way that parents can stimulate the preschool child's interest, is through conversations between parent and child. In parent-child discussions a child can be given lessons in having regard for facts when forming opinions and in having respect for differing viewpoints.

A child can be taught to say, "I think, . . . something is so . . . ," or "So far as I know . . . this is the case." Too many children are "positive" in the full meaning of the old definition—"to be wrong at the top of one's voice." If he criticizes a playmate's actions, for example, there is an opportunity to examine with him why he reacted as he did, decide if he is justified in his feelings or not, and consider if he should emulate or avoid similar behavior.

As has been pointed out before, parents should not try to impose standards of quality or neatness in activities that are beyond the child's capacity. If parents are too demanding, the child will become discouraged. Give a minimum of advice and a good deal of praise for inventiveness and achievement. One boy refused to take home any of his drawings. "Even if Mother likes what I made," he explained, "she'll look to see how neatly I wrote my name or find something that's not perfect enough for her. I just can't please her a hundred per cent."

It is worth while to set standards and make demands, however, when it comes to keeping materials in their proper place and cleaning up after the work is done. Scraps of paper should be picked up, scissors should be put away, pencils and crayons belong in their boxes, and the working area should be tidied up. In this way the child begins to learn good working habits and self-discipline.

Every child appreciates praise and a well-placed compliment is an important means of encouragement. Another is to have a bulletin board in the child's room or in some corner that won't interfere with the interior decorating. Here can be pinned up his pastings and drawings for admiration now and then by adults. One grandmother mounts her grandchildren's drawings on a bulletin board over her bathtub.

Parents should not be particularly concerned with which specific activities capture their child's attention, since almost all serve the same purpose. They encourage a child to learn, enable him to share experiences with his parents, develop his powers of observation and description, and train him to be accurate in dealing with facts.

A child may not be capable of some of these activities until he is virtually of school age or older. Others, in simplified form, may be undertaken by the younger child. For example, while a four-year-old may not be able to write about his trip to the zoo, he can always relate what he has seen—in fact, it will probably be impossible to keep him from doing so. If the family has a tape recorder, he can use that to record his experiences. If there is a typewriter in the house, the older child may use it to practice new words, while the younger child taps out letters and learns to identify them.

Phonograph records can be an excellent introduction to literature and music. Children's stories and poems have been recorded. Some children's favorite is a recording of Bible stories. There are musical compositions by well-known composers that are intended for children and give them an introduction to the sounds different musical instruments make. Well-known examples are *Peter and the Wolf* by the Russian composer, Sergei Prokofiev, *The Young Person's Guide to the Orchestra* by Benjamin Britten, the English composer, and the *Toy Symphony* by Joseph Haydn, with its clever use of everyday sounds, such as bird whistles. The development of unbreakable records makes it practical to give a child discs of his own. As soon as a child is old enough to manipulate it, an inexpensive record player can be a welcome gift.

Through listening to music and learning the sounds made by different musical instruments, the child may become interested in learning to play an instrument himself. Before parents let themselves believe they have a future concert performer on their hands, they should allow the child to test his interest on a rented or borrowed instrument, if possible, or acquire an inexpensive one.

Even when a child does seem genuinely interested in learning to play a musical instrument, many parents become more concerned about the activity than about the child. Such parents insist on long practice sessions even when the child prefers to give much of the time to outdoor play. Often they express disappointment if the child does not develop rapidly into an accomplished performer.

As a result of such pressure, which makes what should be an interesting activity into an onerous duty, many children rebel against learning to play a musical instrument. Since it requires a great deal of diligence and effort to learn to play an instrument well, parents should not push a child too hard in the beginning, but allow time to let interest in music grow.

A parent who would like to give a child the chance to try a musical instrument without investing in the usual piano or violin, might offer the child something as comparatively simple and inexpensive as a recorder. An early version of the flute, a fairly good recorder can be had for less than twenty dollars. It is comparatively easy to learn to play fairly well, and many pretty and simple tunes have been written for it by noted composers of the past. If a parent plays the piano, the two can soon be playing simple tunes together.

One of the most common and worth-while parent-child activities is to take excursions to local places of interest. Where the child is taken will depend on how old he is. One of the first visits, of course, will be to the zoo, if your city has one. Museums are another standard visiting place when they are available.

Some parents worry because there are no such facilities in

the smaller towns in which they live. While such communities do lack some of the facilities of large cities, they have certain advantages of their own. The kind of outdoor life available to the small-town child, and the knowledge he can acquire through it, is denied the city child. In a small community, a child can roam more freely, he usually has more space to indulge his hobbies, and he can find substitutes for the experiences he misses. If there are no picture galleries, for example, there are many fine books of painting reproductions now available. The automobile allows weekend trips to a nearby city to fill in the learning experiences not available at home.

In addition to the usual places to take children, parents should not neglect what they may consider commonplace sights. To every young child, they are brand new. For example, father's place of work, whether office, store, or factory, is always exciting to a child. Local industries, construction projects, department and specialty stores, banks and bridges, are interesting to a child. All boys love trains. The local terminal, switching yard, or station is an exciting sight to them. Take both boys and girls to local scenic wonders, such as caves, canyons, mountains. Don't overlook tunnels, and, of course, airports. City hall and the local courthouse are sights at which even adult citizens might often have a closer look. Visiting these places is a thrilling experience for the child becoming acquainted with the world beyond his own street and his own neighborhood. In making these trips, children often prefer having a companion of their own age and sex along with whom to share the experience.

On these excursions, parents might keep in mind a definition of the function of education by Nicholas Murray Butler, one of the country's most distinguished University Presidents: "To make the obvious more meaningful."

While most gifted children make friends easily, many of

these activities can be useful in helping a shy child make friends. Just as with adults, common interests help bridge the first difficult steps in meeting others. Places where other parents bring their children are often good places for children to develop their social skills.

As was pointed out before, if a boy is having difficulty keeping up with his playmates in games, some help from father can often improve him enough to enjoy playing with the others. It has already been noted that a gifted boy may need extra encouragement in games because he finds he does not master them as quickly as intellectual activities. Somehow, the athletically gifted are usually excused if it turns out that they are not quite up to the average intellectually. But the intellectually gifted child is sometimes mocked if he is not at least as good as most of the others in sports.

No child should be forced to play a game he does not like or cannot play well enough to enjoy. Athletic activities are varied enough in the skills they require for a boy to find some he will like and in which he can do reasonably well.

While learning to do fairly well in athletics can sometimes be a problem for young boys, girls usually do not have this problem. Their games are less demanding and less competitive.

During the preschool period, many of the learning experiences of gifted girls and boys are similar. The principles and activities that have been discussed can be applied to both. Girls and boys need the same incentives and motivation to learn, they are learning the same basic intellectual skills, and they are becoming acquainted with the same outside world.

At the same time, of course, they are learning differing attitudes and engaging in different activities based on the fact that they are either boys or girls. Some of their special interests will depend on their sex. A boy will imitate his father's mannerisms and want to share his special interests, such as fishing. A girl will model herself after her mother, trying on her high-heeled slippers and imitating some of her housekeeping activities.

Still, as a gifted child, a boy and a girl have the same basic needs. Whether boy or girl, the gifted preschool child is learning his first lessons about the world and getting ready for the most important activity of childhood—going to school.

CHAPTER EIGHT

The Gifted Child in School

"NOW THAT PETER is starting school," his mother said on the first day of the term, "we can leave the rest to you experts. We've done our part. Now his teachers can take over."

Many parents share the opinion of Peter's mother. A class of gifted children was questioned as to how many were told by their parents that they should save questions for the teacher rather than raise them at home. All but a few stated their parents expected the school to do all of the academic teaching.

As one boy said, "If I start asking questions, Dad tells me, 'Find out at school. That's the place to learn and your teachers are paid to help you.'"

This boy's father was only partly right. It is, of course, the teacher's job to help children. But the school is only one of the places where children learn. The home is equally important. In most instances, where the elementary school has no special facilities or program for the gifted, the home is in certain ways even more important as an institution of learning than the school. The gifted pupils in such schools must learn some of their most important academic lessons at home.

A gifted child's mind does not stop working when he

walks out of the classroom. Therefore his parents should not expect him to restrict his efforts to learn only to school hours. If the gifted child's classroom assignments are below the level of his knowledge and ability, his mind can actually get its best chances to function at its own level outside the classroom. He is in school about five hours a day. Parents are responsible for the other nineteen hours.

In a crowded classroom a teacher cannot do as much as she wishes for the gifted child. Much of her attention must be given to those who are less able. Even in a class made up entirely of the gifted she can give only a fraction of her time to each child. Yet each of these children has enough curiosity and is brimming with enough questions to occupy a large part of a teacher's attention all by himself.

The gifted child, therefore, can profitably use more attention and more time than any teacher is likely to give him. If he is fortunate, he will receive this additional help from his parents.

From such parents he will get the continuing encouragement he needs in order to keep his mind working at the level of which it is capable, rather than at the lower standard set for the class. His parents will continue developing his motivation to learn and his pride in achievement. They will help him explore new interests and maintain high standards of workmanship.

Parents who fill their gifted child's needs for such intellectual stimulation are helping him prepare for later years, when he will face the kind of intellectual demands his mind is capable of meeting. At one time it was thought that the gifted could safely coast through their early schooling. When they finally reached a point where they had to make an effort to meet an intellectual challenge, it was believed, the gifted could simply rouse their dozing faculties and successfully tackle their studies.

Research studies have shown this is not true. Psychologists

have found that in some ways the mind is like a muscle. Unused, it grows flabby. Untrained, it cannot handle difficult problems.

Scholarship, like sports, requires that those who want to do well must keep in training. Baseball players, for example, must keep in condition. While their skills are still developing, they do their "studying" in the minor leagues, where they learn and practice their fundamentals.

Students need similar training and seasoning. A child, even if highly gifted, must learn how to learn and then practice on problems that "exercise" his mind if he intends to go on to advanced studies. If the classwork is not particularly demanding, he can probably get along by only half trying. But half-way efforts will not be adequate in a good high school, and certainly not in college. By that time, unless he has had opportunities to use his full abilities, he may not be able to meet the higher academic standards. Not having learned how to study and concentrate, his mind will literally be out of practice.

Parents often complain that the school has not taught their child how to study. In a special sense the old saying about leading a horse to water holds true in such a case. If a child is not thirsty, you cannot make him drink. Parents must seek to provide the salt that will create the thirst for knowledge.

The child whose mind has not been stimulated and trained all through his childhood will probably not even want to make the required effort once he finds that the schoolwork has gotten too demanding for him to learn without trying. He will not have developed the motivation to achieve and the pride in accomplishment that a child must have in order to persist in difficult studies. Part of the parents' task, therefore, is to fill the gap between what the classroom requires of the gifted child and what the gifted child actually requires in order to promote the proper development of his abilities.

Filling the gap, however, requires a great deal more than just supplementing a child's school work with home assignments. A child's mind is not separate from the rest of the child. The fact that a child is gifted affects every aspect of his development. Helping a gifted mind to grow is therefore part of the over-all task of helping the whole child to grow—physically, emotionally, spiritually, and socially—as well as intellectually.

Because of his special abilities, the gifted child should not have intellectual activities so overstressed that physical activities are neglected. The child should be encouraged to have normal social relationships with children of his age. Because he may be a good deal older than his years intellectually, he should not be expected to be equally mature emotionally. At the same time, because his mind is advanced, spiritual questions are likely to trouble him earlier and more deeply than they do average children. To these questions he will need sympathetic and satisfying answers from his parents.

Fundamentally, therefore, the difference in the task facing the parents of the school-age child as compared to the preschool years is that now they have assistance from trained teachers. They cannot, however, give over the whole job of promoting the child's development to the school while they concern themselves principally with keeping the child fed and clothed and getting him to school on time. They should continue through the school years their preschool program of fostering the child's interests, providing him with the opportunities to explore them, and keeping the various aspects of his development in balance as that he may grow into a mature individual.

Once the gifted child has entered school, many parents believe the best way they can then aid his development is to see that he does as much homework as possible. If they find he completes his assignments quickly, or perhaps does not even get any drill to do at home, they feel the teacher is neglecting him.

Many parents show up at school insisting their child be given more arithmetic problems to solve or more spelling lists to write out. "My girl finishes her work so quickly," one mother complained. "I'm sure she's not getting enough work to do. Can't you give her bigger assignments?"

This mother had put her finger on the right problem, but she suggested the wrong solution. Her little girl was bright enough to whip through her class assignments quickly. But giving her more of the same kind of work to do would not benefit the child. Many parents make the mistake of thinking that repetitious drill, even when not needed, serves as a form of "mental discipline." Instead of disciplining the gifted child, however, purposeless repetition can make a bright child rebellious. He is smart enough to see he is wasting his time.

Children who find their school work almost too easy for their own good do not need more drill in what they can already do perfectly. They need work that is more advanced and more varied. An increasing number of schools are providing such "enriched" programs for gifted children. Unfortunately, the vast majority of schools cannot. This is where parents must step in.

Parents should give their child the opportunity to go further with his learning than is possible in school. For example, a teacher facing the prospect of reading and correcting thirty student essays may ask the class to confine their reports to one or two pages. One father, however, made it his business to read his girl's paper and then ask, "What more would you have said if you had more space?" The child was thus encouraged to do more research than was required, since she knew she would have an audience to whom to report.

Whatever subject comes easily to a child can thus be kept interesting and challenging for him by giving him the opportunity to explore it more thoroughly. Instead of spelling the same words over and over, parents can help a child learn new words by changing prefixes and suffixes, and by looking up synonyms. Similarly with arithmetic, or any other subject.

An equally valuable way for a child to use the free time he has left when assignments are done quickly, or he has no assignments to do, is in exploring his own hobbies or special interests. For doing his work well the youngster is thereby rewarded with the chance to pursue whatever other interest he wishes. Such time can be given to listening to music, playing a musical instrument, reading the book of his choice, watching an occasional television program.

Only part of the gifted child's spare time should be concentrated on intellectual activities. Over-enrichment of the intellectual diet can be as harmful as an over-rich diet at the dining room table. Either form of stuffing produces its own kind of indigestion.

A gifted youngster, like any other child, needs time to play, to relax, to do nothing at all. Parents should be wary of pushing the child too hard, of always making demands for still higher achievement, of never expressing satisfaction with his accomplishments.

Some parents use money rewards as an incentive for high marks. The result is to give the child the wrong goal. Instead of seeking to learn for the satisfaction of gaining knowledge, he looks for an immediate reward. One father, for example, asked his boy why his arithmetic marks went up one month, when he had been promised a fountain pen if he achieved a certain grade, and right down again the next month. "Well," the child replied, "I didn't need any more fountain pens."

Psychologists have shown that the most lasting motivation to learn comes from personal pride in achievement, not from some immediate material reward. Parents can build up this kind of motivation by expressing their approval of their child's efforts to explore new fields of knowledge.

A question perplexing many parents of gifted children is whether or not to approve of their child skipping a grade. At one time skipping, or "acceleration," was considered the simple and obvious solution for the child who was far ahead of his classmates. Then opinion changed and many considered it harmful for a child to be pushed into a group in which his age and size might prevent him from being accepted by his new classmates. The shift of opinion from one extreme to the other kept back many children who would have profited from acceleration.

Today, skipping is again receiving increased support from many educators. Others, however, insist the proper way to handle the advanced student is to keep him with his age group and enrich his study program with additional learning opportunities.

Enrichment is the primary method used at Hunter, but in certain cases children may also be accelerated. In some school programs, however, enrichment does not mean more variety in learning opportunities but simply more of the same. The gifted pupil may then find himself doing twice as much of the same thing as his classmates. When the gifted child has no genuine opportunity to use his abilities if he stays with his age group, acceleration may be desirable.

In many schools there is a firm policy regarding skipping and the parent has no choice. The child will be skipped or not, as the rules dictate. But fairly often the parents are asked to decide whether their child should be accelerated a grade. Then they often ponder worriedly, wondering which choice to make. If the child skips, will he find himself without friends? If he doesn't skip, will he lose valuable intellectual benefits? Which is more important in the long run?

In trying to decide, parents should consider the following points:

1. The child's physical development.

If a child is large and well built for his age, perhaps even above average, it will be easier for him to adjust socially to an older group than if he is small or undersized. A very young child's size and comparative strength is important in determining whether older children will accept him as a playmate. These considerations are less important in secondary school.

2. The child's social development.

The age of the child's present play group and the position he holds in it are important indicators of how he will fare if he is skipped into an older group. If he is already playing with older children, there is obviously no problem. If he is a leader in his own group, he is probably sufficiently advanced to adjust to an older group. However, if the child is shy with children of his own age, or has difficulty getting along with them, things will probably be even harder with an older group.

Social poise can be even more important than physical size in determining whether a child can make the jump from his own age group to the next. For example, a child who was small for his age was skipped to the next class in his school. For a while he had difficulty in gaining acceptance from the older children. But he was a friendly, helpful child, who started giving assistance to some of the children in his new class who were having difficulty with their work. He began making friends and eventually he was completely accepted. On the other hand, a girl who was as large and advanced as her new classmates had a great deal of difficulty because of emotional immaturity. Comments by her new classmates which she wrongly interpreted as criticisms made her burst into tears. Seeking approval, she began running to the teacher to report on other pupils. Soon she found herself almost friendless, although acceptance had been easy at first.

3. The frequency with which children in the school are accelerated.

If acceleration is the school's standard policy for handling superior pupils, the chances are better that the child will find companions in his new grade. Also, he is less likely to seem out of place, since accelerated pupils are more accepted throughout the school.

Acceleration has lately become more widespread in the country's school system at all levels. For example, scholarships are being awarded to gifted high school students so that they can enter college after two years of high school. On the whole, therefore, it would seem that if the parent is given a choice, and there is no good reason for not accelerating the child, he should probably be allowed to move ahead.

Whether or not a school has special facilities for the gifted, parents can often contribute to an enrichment program for the school. One way to do this is to help the school acquire materials for which the budget does not provide.

The parents of gifted children can join together and see that the school library has subscriptions to magazines to which it would normally not subscribe, but which serve the interests of the gifted. Special publications on music and hobbies are examples. Similarly, contributions to the library of books from which the gifted might be expected to benefit is another way of helping the school enrich its program for the gifted.

Parents groups should always consult with teachers or the principal to learn what kind of assistance would be most valuable and what contributions are most desired. One parent circulated a letter to all of the parents in her child's class listing all of the items—mostly materials useful for arts-and-crafts activities—that the teacher had said she could use for the class. Each mother checked off items she could supply and suggested additional items for the teacher's approval, to be requested by her if they could be used.

Another parent assembled a list of places that small groups of children could visit by special arrangement. She sent it to other parents who added to it the businesses with which the fathers were connected that children might be interested in visiting. Still another way to enrich the school program is for the parents who are working in fields that might interest children to make themselves available upon request to give talks about their specialities.

Whatever else they may do, parents should do their best to attend school functions to which they are invited. They should also perform without delay the small duties, such as filling out forms, that schools require on occasion. Because of their sensitivity to others' feelings and opinions, gifted children are deeply concerned that teachers and fellow pupils should not think their parents are neglectful of them. They will often take the blame themselves for their parents' forgetfulness or make excuses for their parents' failure to appear at a school function.

At one class party to celebrate Mother's Day, every child but one sat beside his mother. Every time the door opened, Danny turned eagerly. Then, disappointed, he looked down at the empty place beside him. Finally his hand moved slowly to the place card put there for his mother and he slipped it into his pocket. The teacher seated herself in the empty chair and Danny looked up gratefully. He hesitated for a moment and then an "explanation" gushed out. "It's my mother's birthday and some of her friends are giving her a party. But she said she would try to leave early and come. I guess she couldn't make it."

One little girl, whose own work was always done on time, was usually late with papers that her parents had to sign. She would make the apology, "I forgot to bring it," or, if a more elaborate explanation seemed called for, "It was too late when I remembered that you wanted my father to answer your note," but her face betrayed her embarrassment.

Parents who want to enlarge the variety of activities available to the gifted can form afterschool groups. This enables a child to spend time with other children who have common interests but need not be the same age. Some parents of gifted children have formed groups to provide lessons in typing, foreign languages, art, science, and other subjects. Contributions from each parent enable them to hire special teachers. A parent with special background or training may serve as the teacher.

Parents who want to encourage their children to bring friends home will have to resign themselves to the fact that children inevitably upset a room to some extent. They will have to be prepared to accept a certain amount of noisiness and disorder no matter how well-intentioned the children may be.

One of the best ways to keep a group of children in hand is to provide them with a play area in which they cannot do any serious damage. Then keep them occupied with plenty of materials, such as paper, paint, scraps of cloth, and any similar odds and ends that are available and which they can use as they wish. A favorite occupation is to make a collage, in which they combine as many differently textured materials as they can.

Every group of children has one member in whose home they prefer to congregate. The following comments were made by children who were asked why they preferred to visit certain homes:

"It is friendly at Joe's house. His mother is a wonderful hostess who thinks up swell things for us to do."

"You don't have to be careful where, how, and why you put down things. Mrs. Smith knows that children can be careless sometimes, but not mean to be."

"Tom's dad has hospitality and good manners. He is the same to kids that he is to grownups."

"There is a nice atmosphere at Ann's house. They always seem to be prepared for us."

"Barbara's mother sits down with us and we make little doodads. She has such good ideas when we run out of them."

"Harold has many games in a big box, and we can pull out any of them if we put them back before we leave. He has stacks of records, too, and no one says, 'Be careful. Don't break them.'"

"Mrs. Savarese has a big chest full of costumes and old jewelry, and stuff that we can use to make our own costumes. She puts in shoes with high heels, too, and isn't afraid we'll break our necks if we wear them."

Parents interested in forming children's groups will find that the following ages usually get along best together: 5 to 8, 8 to 11, 11 to 13. Above 13, age grouping is less important than common interests.

The gifted child should not always be kept in the company of the gifted. He needs to learn how to get along with his fellows, no matter what their intellectual abilities. For this purpose, such organizations as the Cub Scouts, Boy and Girl Scouts, Campfire Girls, and 4-H Clubs are valuable. They enable the gifted child to diversify his interests and make more friends.

The gifted child often learns his first lessons in getting along with other children in his own home, as he works out a way of living peacefully with the other children in the family. Sometimes all of the children in a family are gifted, sometimes one or more, but not all. Gifted or not, however, the squabbles between older and younger children are nearly always over the same causes. The older child does not want the younger to use his playthings. The younger child wants to stay up as late as the older. Every parent is familiar with these disputes.

The advantage in dealing with a gifted child is that it is usually easier to reason with him. He will understand why he must do certain things and probably obey more readily. But, like all children, a certain amount of grumbling should be expected from any child who has to do something he does not like.

Few parents favor one child over another, but impose the same sensible regulations and discipline whether the child is gifted or not. This eliminates one reason for children's battles, since children bitterly resent what they interpret as favoritism or special privilege shown to another.

While most parents are wary of making this mistake, they sometimes make another. They will compare the children's grades and reproach the child who is apparently doing poorly. Not infrequently, it is the gifted child who gets the rebuke because he appears not to be doing as well as the child known to have less ability.

Parents often do not realize that many report cards give ratings based on how well the teacher thinks the child is doing in terms of his own ability rather than in comparison with other children. The gifted child may be accomplishing a great deal more than the less capable child, but his teacher may decide he is not doing as well as he can and therefore grade him accordingly. Whether or not the teacher is correct in her estimate, the situation is not improved by criticizing one child's achievement in front of the other. A likely consequence is the development of antagonism between the children. It should also be remembered that teachers have individual standards and one may not be grading on the same basis as the other.

Parents would do best if they simply make it a general rule not to compare one child's grades or achievements with the others', even if all are gifted. Although they should all have similar rules of discipline, comparable household responsibilities, and equivalent privileges, they should be treated as individuals when it comes to their interests, their activities, and their achievements. Gifted or not, suitable methods of stimulating interests, encouraging achievement, and building motivation to learn should be applied to all of the children in a family. But it should not be expected that each child will respond in the same way to the same techniques and teachers. Once a child is given the opportunities he requires, he should then be allowed to progress at the pace set by his individual capacities.

A special problem may arise if children from the same family attend the same school and the school suggests accelerating one and not the other. It is not fair to the better student to keep him back. Yet the other must be made to feel he, too, has special abilities.

One mother confronted with this problem told her two daughters, "Jill is good in books, but Jane is good in music, so I shall get her the violin she has been wanting and arrange for lessons." This mother realized that when one child is singled out for special attention the other should also be given a distinction in some way.

A younger child who may be more gifted than an older child should never, if it can be avoided, be allowed in the same class with the older. Rather than let this happen, it is even advisable, if possible, to place the children in different schools, where different methods and schedules will lessen the appearance of direct competition between them.

Twins should usually be separated if two classes are available. The two children will rarely be equally gifted, yet the teacher is likely to expect the same work from both. Even when their level of ability is the same, their temperaments and ways of doing things will differ and they should be considered as individuals rather than duplicates. Each should be encouraged to develop independent interests rather than the two of them forced to develop as one unit.

Although the child has been learning, building his personality, developing attitudes, and thus forming patterns of behavior from his earliest days, it is in the early school years that his behavior patterns are established. Parents who have been working with their gifted child all along will continue building on the foundation they have constructed. But it would be valuable for them to keep certain new considerations in mind.

For example, the child is now old enough to mingle more frequently with adults. Proud parents who show off their child's ability to tinkle a piano or recite verses have been cartooned so often that most parents avoid doing so, but they often encourage another form of exhibitionism. This is demonstrated by the child who proudly prattles newly acquired tidbits of knowledge.

The kind of child who is probably most cordially disliked by adults is the one who expects them to stop their conversation and listen to everything he has to say with the same rapt attention his parents give him. Parents should teach children that at most gatherings of adults they should be seen for a short while, heard briefly, and leave the room.

Children themselves will usually prefer this. Most of them get restless and impatient if they have to stay in adult company—except for favorite relatives and friends—more than a little while. It is usually when they get bored and restless that they begin seeking attention in the most effective way they know. But when a child knows he will be excused quickly after he exchanges the formalities of greetings and introductions, he will usually extend his best manners for that short period.

The kind of self-restraint a child must learn to exercise in adult company is similar to the good manners he must learn to practice with other children. The gifted child may have to be taught to control his superior abilities and not be impatient, rude, sarcastic, or domineering with other children who are not as mentally quick as he. Gifted children have to be taught that nobody wants to be told he is stupid or inept, no matter how true it may be. This training in self-control will be invaluable for him when he grows older and must learn to work with others and gain their co-operation.

An effective way to restrain the child who may show tendencies to be overbearing as a result of his mental superiority is to have him list the activities he cannot perform well, and that others in his class or play group can, as a balance for those he lists as his special abilities. He needs to be taught that his capabilities are not something to flaunt but a gift he must use modestly and with a sense of responsibility and helpfulness toward others. Children, particularly the gifted, are idealistic. Parents can instill in the child standards of service, thoughtfulness, and concern for others if they will take the time and make the effort.

At the same time, the gifted child's perceptiveness and ability to reason presents parents with the responsibility of practicing as much as possible of what they preach. The gifted child has a clear eye for adult caprices and contradictions. If the child, himself, is disciplined irrationally, sometimes being punished for trifles and sometimes allowed to get away with tantrums; if he sees his parents blithely committing what they describe to him as misdeeds; if he hears them praise or excuse others for actions he is warned are improper; he is certainly less likely to take parental advice seriously.

On the other hand, parents often expect the gifted child to show more maturity than is possible for him. No matter how far beyond his years a gifted child may be in his ability to reason, he will not be advanced much beyond his age in the way he feels. Some parents think their gifted child must be as advanced socially and emotionally as he is intellectually. They become exasperated at a child doing things he should "know" are wrong. One of the most common exclamations heard in such homes is, "Why did you do that? You know better!"

If the parent insists on an explanation for misbehavior that obviously has no satisfactory excuse, the gifted child will probably oblige by manufacturing an excuse and rationalizing his behavior. This only makes matters worse. The parent sees through the effort and thinks the child is being willfully deceitful and disrespectful.

Such a parent would do better if he accepted the fact that every child succumbs to youthful temptations and commits childhood errors. If a child has disobeyed a previously explained directive, the parent should state flatly, "You know better than to do this, for I have explained why you should not. The penalty is—"

Eleven-year-old Arthur revealed that he understood this problem rather well. Filling out a questionnaire that began, "The boy who bothers me most is——because he——" Arthur filled in his own name and wrote:

"Goodness knows that by this time, with all of the talks I've gotten from different teachers, I should know that I am my own worst enemy. It bothers me, and I keep trying to improve, but just when I think I've corrected some bad habit, something happens and there I go again."

One mother showed that she understood well the difference between the levels at which a gifted child thinks and behaves. Her little girl, she noted, was as advanced mentally as an eight- or nine-year-old, but, "She's very six-year-old in most behavior aspects."

In their efforts to discipline and train the gifted, parents start with two advantages. First, the gifted child is more deeply influenced by their opinions and actions than they may realize. In classroom discussions, for example, children often preface their statements with, "My mother told me . . ." or "My father says . . ." They take seriously what they are told at home so long as they believe they are being spoken to honestly.

Second, the gifted child is usually capable of sharp-eyed self-analysis. If he sees one kind of behavior is not getting him what he wants, he will usually change his ways. The parent may be able to use reasonable suggestion or need to employ firm discipline, whichever fits the occasion.

One boy, whose tantrums apparently got him what he wanted at home, tried the same technique in his kindergarten class when he could not have a toy he wanted. Efforts to speak with him only produced louder wails. The teacher took him by the hand and led him into an empty room down the hall.

"Is that the loudest you can cry?" she asked. The sobbing subsided. "Let me hear how well you cry," the teacher persisted. "I think it's very interesting."

The sobs slowed down to a few gulps. "It is not interesting," the child finally retorted. "It's disgusting." He blew his nose and hurried back to his class.

A psychologist who pioneered in the study of giftedness has described the middle school years as possibly the gifted child's most difficult years. This is the time when he becomes more clearly aware of his differences from other children; when he must try to learn how to get along with others, even when they are less able than he; when he must make his adjustments to school and to classroom work that may not be up to his level of ability; when he develops his attitudes toward formal education; when he consciously begins to evaluate himself and the world around him.

Children are often more responsive to adults and thoughtful about the world around them than adults usually realize. And the gifted are even more so than less capable children. Many insights into how gifted children think, and what they think about, have come from the autobiographies each child at Hunter must write at the end of the sixth grade. The first drafts are written in the classroom. Uncensored by the parents, they often reveal unsuspected attitudes toward family and self.

Ellen, who dedicated her autobiography, entitled "Life of

the Youngest Dracula," to James Mason, Bela Lugosi, and
Jean Pierre Aumont, "three family heroes," wrote in her
foreword:

"To all those who don't read forewords, you will understand this autobiography better if you read *this* foreword.

"First my dedication, you may think it odd that I do not
dedicate this autobiography to my family.

"Don't misunderstand, my family did a lot to help me in
life, but they don't need a dedication from me to know my
gratitude."

Examining herself, Ellen notes in her first chapter, entitled
"Born of a Mother":

"I was born in French Hospital at 2:00 A.M. I had a normal weight and was not as skinny as was my sister when she
was born. At that time I did not know my fate was to love
freedom, independence, and fantasy.

"I seemed to be more normal than any of our family. My
sister had been born late and had to have her arm broken at
birth, my brother was born too soon. I was born on time,
with my proper weight and my mother did not have to go
into exhausting labor. She was very happy having me and
I was no trouble. But I was soon to prove different."

The chapter titled, "Oh! Golden Years," shows how the
gifted can learn to accept difficult situations:

"Despite the fact that I was very happy I had one problem. Our housekeeper, Rosalie. She had an awful temper
and the slightest thing made her blow her top. However, I
lived through it and managed to hold on through my sixth
year."

In the chapter, "Trouble with a Wolf," Ellen shows a
startling degree of feminine insight and good-humored
sophistication for her years:

"My ninth summer dawned. We went down to Atlanta. It
was here I first learned the problems of romance and how
to cope with them. The Anderson family consisted of four

boys and a girl. The youngest boy was my age, the next oldest was eleven, the third was at least thirteen, and the fourth I didn't see till quite late in the year.

"I was lonely. My brother always played with Henry, the youngest, and the others, except Jimmy, the third oldest, were happy-go-lucky in the woods all the time. Jimmy spent his time making eyes at me.

"One day when my brother and I were playing with our new toy planes Jack Anderson appeared on the scene. He was the most wonderful boy I had met, or so I thought, and I promptly fell in love with him. Especially after he climbed to the top of the tallest pine tree just to get my plane for me.

"While I enjoyed myself and stuck around Jack who was beginning to like me, Jimmy became very angry and one day locked me in his room and wouldn't let me go until I kissed him. This went on until one day Jack suggested that John and I were in love, to which Jimmy's immediate response was 'No!' Jack promptly knocked him down. Then followed a HORRIBLE FIST FIGHT THAT ENDED THAT AFFAIR."

In a chapter called, "Fast Flying, Not Trying," Ellen described some of her early school experiences and how she learned to take care of herself in a difficult school:

"In Public School in second grade was when I began hardening into what I am today. P.S. — was not a good school, but I made the best of it that I could. I was the quietest and the best student in my class even if it was only because no one but myself really studied. But this did not harden me, what really did was the fact that everyone yelled and screamed even when the teacher was there.

"After lunch we were shoved out of the building only to be herded like cattle by monitors into long lines. The girls were all in one line on one side of the school doors, the boys on the other. The monitors wouldn't even let you talk no matter how much they talked, and to eat even the tiniest piece of candy was a sin, even if they could eat lollypops and ice-cream cones. But there were a few who managed to escape the monitors for a little while. I was usually one of these, and had an enjoyable time chasing the boys for chasing the other girls, even though the other girls never accepted me as a friend."

In her chapter, "Growing, Growing, Growing," Ellen shows how the years brought greater self-awareness and new interests:

"It was in my tenth year that things began to dawn on me. Up till that time I had taken things as the facts of life but I couldn't overlook certain things forever. For instance I was very strong for my age. I was also very fast on my feet and a very good jumper too.

"I liked tigers and other jungle animals very much, and I read every book about them I could get my paws on. I soon began to act kind of tigerish too. My brother and I made up a game in which we acted like wild animals, and I still like to grow my fingernails very long.

"I soon took to reading a great deal of fantasy books and I grew to like vampires very much, so naturally one night, after my eleventh birthday I stayed up to watch 'Dracula.'"

Bringing her life up to date, Ellen concludes:

"And so as soon as I graduate I will have completed my responsibilities up to this point. I hope my future will be happy."

Ellen is not a typical gifted child. In the truest sense every child is unique and Ellen is even more so than most children. But her autobiography does illustrate the insight, the individuality, and the quality of thought revealed by many gifted children.

Gifted children can often see through sham as clearly as the youngster in "The Emperor's New Clothes." But they are usually clever enough to be cautious in expressing themselves. After kindergarten, it is almost impossible to persuade them to discuss the classmates they dislike, perhaps because they distrust the way adults would use the information and fear possible retaliation by those whose names they would give. However, researchers have used a variety of techniques to learn what kinds of behavior school-age children dislike in their fellows and the results provide a worthwhile check list of the characteristics children dislike in each other.

In any group of children, gifted or not, one or two have few friends and find it difficult to make new ones. When moved to a new class, in the hope that a fresh start will help them do better, they usually show again the traits that caused them to be rejected in the previous class.

One trait that will cause such rejection is the use of physical violence. Some children will punch, kick, or pinch to get what they want. Soon the other children stop going near them.

Others, a little older, will scramble around the room while their classmates are trying to work or are playing in small groups. They may shout when others are quiet, drawing cold looks or verbal reproofs from the others. The other youngsters consider them "wild" or "noisy and nosy."

One such six-year-old, who responded neither to the teacher nor his fellows, was analyzed for the teacher by a classmate. "He is completely unmanageable. Just watch him when his mother calls for him after school, and you'll see he is ten times worse with her than with you. He hits her and she hits him back until she sees the other mothers looking at her. Then she calls a taxi to get him out of sight in a hurry, but she should call the taxi first and hit him when they get home."

Seven-year-olds will misbehave less conspicuously. Those disliked by their classmates are described as "touchy," "fussy," and "rude."

Eight-year-olds dislike their fellows whom they deem

"tattletales" and "mamma's precious baby." The latter are
often described by the other children as those who "dish it
out but can't take it."

Nine- and ten-year-olds have usually learned to conform
to group standards of behavior. Those who do not get along
are likely to be described as "sly," "sneaky," or "undercover
guys."

The eleven-year-olds often use picturesque phrases to describe the unpopular. "He is too bullyish for me." "She has
a split personality, for she likes me one moment and the next
she doesn't." "He tells me what is wrong with me and that I
make him sick. Then he tells me how wonderful he is in kick
ball."

Parents observing their child may not see any signs of
such traits or not be aware of characteristics that other children find distasteful. As a result, they may not be able to
understand why a child may have difficulty in making and
keeping friends. These traits are more likely to show up at
home when there is more than one child in the family. By
observing how children get along with each other within the
home, how well they fare with their playmates, and by learning from teachers how successfully they are accepted by
classmates, parents can get an idea of the child's ability to
relate to others. Once parents have this knowledge, they can
work on the characteristics that need improving.

A characteristic the gifted occasionally show is often mis-
interpreted by parents. This is the storytelling in which a
gifted child may indulge. Highly imaginative children may
describe as true some incidents that happened only in their
own minds. They do not bother to distinguish between make-
believe stories and true ones.

Their stories may be recited in a straightforward manner
that completely deceives the stranger. Although the child
pretends to be relating an actual occurrence, so many details
are pure fiction that the informed listener thinks the child is

deliberately lying. More likely, he is only expressing his unfulfilled wishes or using stories as a way to express his imagination.

A teacher invited to dinner by Larry's mother commended her for allowing the boy to go on his vacation trip the previous summer. "It was good for him to have such an unusual experience," she noted. Larry reddened and his mother appeared startled. "What was so unusual about it?" she asked.

The teacher looked surprised. "It's not every child who goes out to the Far West and lives with relatives who have homesteads in that part of the country. The class was certainly interested to hear about his experiences, and he described them vividly."

When the teacher had left, Larry's mother asked, "Why did you make up such a story?"

The boy looked shamefaced. "Every fall our teachers ask what we did during vacation and some of the other kids tell about exciting things that happened to them and I never have anything interesting to tell. You told me so much about your aunt and uncle out West that it seemed like I'd been there. Anyway, it was more interesting to talk about than what happened at day camp."

The child who makes up stories is expressing an inner need. The attentive parent, by listening to these stories, can often gain a better understanding of the child.

Often, children make up stories about what they would like to be when they grow up. Even though gifted children rarely make final vocational choices at this age, the extent of their ambition is already being formed. Parents are usually the most important influence in giving children the ambition to go to college. If parents treat higher education as something they expect a child to achieve, no matter what his specific vocational goals, the child will very likely take the same view.

Of the approximately two thousand children who have completed the sixth grade at the Hunter School, so far as is known every one has entered college. Few have dropped out before getting a degree. In many cases the child's giftedness gave his parents the incentive to make the financial sacrifice of saving up for his education. Once the parents made this decision, their plans and encouragement motivated the child to continue his schooling.

One mother, a hairdresser, said, "No one in my family or my husband's ever went beyond high school. All of them went to work as soon as they were old enough. But I've been hearing other parents plan for college and my boy is as smart as their children. So I'm working extra hours, and every bit of that money goes into the bank for his college education."

The child who accepts a college education as part of his future life will plan his high school program so as to make sure it makes him eligible for college. In this way the motivation and goals are built up that will guide the gifted child in a straight path despite the conflicting noneducational interests and new distractions that come with adolescence and are part of growing up.

CHAPTER NINE

After School Hours

THE MOST IMPORTANT activity for the school-age child is, of course, school itself. Once in school, the gifted child has an important new influence on his learning and his interests. How effective the school will be in teaching the child, in promoting his interest in learning, in inspiring him to explore diversified fields of knowledge depends to a large extent on the quality of the school program.

The attention that elementary schools give the gifted varies enormously. A few schools give special attention to the study and education of gifted children. A growing number of elementary schools not only serve the average children of their area, but also provide special enrichment programs for the gifted. Some schools do little for the gifted except to accelerate them. And most schools, unfortunately, still do almost nothing for them except to give lip service to their needs.

The kind of afterschool activities a child finds most helpful will often depend on the program he is receiving at school. A child advanced in his school subjects, who may spend much of his class time waiting for others to catch up, may need some advanced homework to maintain his interest in schooling. A child whose advanced standing is recognized and who is given suitable assignments in school may do better by exploring different interests at home.

In neither case, however, can parents automatically decide what afterschool activities best suit their child. The best guidance on what the child needs will come from the school and from the child.

First, try to learn from the school what kind of program the child is receiving and to what extent it seems to meet his needs. Since the child's teacher spends a great deal of time with him, she is likely to know the subjects in which he is strong or weak, what special aptitudes or interests he has shown, and what afterschool activities he might find most profitable. The teacher may be able to suggest where certain afterschool activities are offered. Other school personnel, such as a guidance counselor or the school principal, may also be helpful. Don't neglect to query other instructors, such as the child's Sunday-school teacher or camp director.

Second, learn from the child, himself, what he does in school, how his time is occupied, to what extent he is kept busy or left unsatisfied. From his questions while he does his homework assignments, and from the speed with which he does them, it is possible to gain an idea of how he is doing and what more you might do for him. In addition, his comments and questions are a guide to his current interests and help indicate how they might be stimulated and encouraged.

Be wary, at the same time, of accepting at face value a child's statement that he is "bored" in school or that his teacher is not "interesting." Some teachers do not recognize or understand the gifted and such criticisms may at times be deserved. But children can also play for undeserved sympathy or purposely offer the response that gains attention and concern. Teachers are not television entertainers. Some will always be more stimulating than others. The question is not whether the child is kept amused but whether he is being suitably taught. The effectiveness of the teaching that the child receives is what the parents should seek to determine. On the basis of what they find out, parents can then help their child pursue worth-while afterschool activities.

Most gifted children appreciate the qualities of a gifted teacher. One child commented about a past teacher, "Miss Calvert had a wonderful way with little boys. She seemed to know just how much trouble a fellow could find." Another noted: "Our teacher introduced us to many new things. She tried hard to sugar-coat reading, writing, and arithmetic."

Many of the gifted child's school-age interests are a continuation on an advanced level of activities he began before entering school. Probably the best example of this are the more advanced books he will now desire and use.

While the preschool child rarely advances much beyond picture books, perhaps with some text, or simple readers if he is further advanced, the school-age gifted child will begin branching out in his reading as his skill rapidly improves. As soon as he is capable of using them, he should have a simple illustrated dictionary and a junior edition of an atlas. For older children, a world almanac and a thesaurus are valuable additions to his personal library. If possible an encyclopedia suitable for children should be given him.

As he receives these books he should be shown how to use them and taught to look up information on his own. This does not mean a child can be provided with his own little reference library and abandoned in it to find his own way. Parents will still have to provide aid and guidance in looking up information and in interpreting material. "Let's see what the source book says about it," should now become a household byword.

Parents often inquire how to encourage a child's interest in a subject to continue after he first expresses curiosity about it. The basic principle is quite simple. Usually you begin with the child's own questions as a start.

If he is brushed off with a curt reply, his curiosity is not likely to be aroused further in that direction. If, however, he is not only given an answer, but complimented for thinking of the question, he is much more likely to look further into a subject.

"That's a good question," one father would say when his boy seemed to be getting interested in a subject and raised some queries about it. "Why don't you first see how much you can find out on your own, and then we'll look into it together?" Such a technique should not become a device for keeping a child occupied until a later time. It should be part of a genuine demonstration of interest and participation on the parent's part.

One father made it his business to inquire of his son when he came home in the evening, "Have you read anything good today?" If the youngster said he had, the father would glance through it rapidly to show his interest. Later they would spend a few minutes discussing what the boy had been reading.

One little girl became interested in chairs. Her mother took her to the local museum and showed her that chairs were considered works of art and that their design differed in many details. The youngster began her own study of the subject. She learned to identify the periods in which different designs had appeared. As she traced the development of chairs, learning they were once reserved for the use of nobility, she learned history. Most important, she learned how much fascination there can be in researching one's special interests.

Boys and girls are likely to share many of the same interests until adolescence. To adults, it often seems that the girls are even more interested in boy's activities than in those that are expected to interest them. It is not that gifted girls are unusual, but that adults make the mistake of thinking that a young girl's interests will not extend beyond dolls and playing house. If not influenced by adult pressure, the school-age girl is likely to have as wide a variety of interests as the gifted boy of her age.

In trying to select books to serve and stimulate a child's interests, parents often do not realize how wide a variety of desirable publications are available. Besides the reference books already mentioned, an anthology of poetry should be added to the child's library when he is six or seven. The child should also, if possible, have at least one comprehensive work that deals with each of the subject areas he is studying in school. Interesting surveys in science, history, geography, and other fields are available to carry a gifted child beyond what the classroom is likely to offer him. They will help to interest him in learning more about his school subjects.

The enormous variety of books available in paper-bound editions has made it much easier and far less expensive to provide a child with books of his own. The Bible, Shakespeare's plays, poetry, manuals, and scientific works are all available in inexpensive form. Some of the money saved by buying these economy editions should go for a few beautifully printed and illustrated volumes whose attractiveness does much to induce their fortunate young possessors to read and treasure them.

Special magazines for young people on science, history, and other subjects are being published. Profusely illustrated and attractively designed, they are a strong inducement to learn more about the subject they cover.

A child's reading is often stimulated by some other experience, such as a visit to a place of interest. As the child grows older, museums will continually have more to offer him. The utensils, armor, and various other objects produced in the past will probably interest a boy more than the paintings. Mummies, Indian tepees, stuffed animals are all new and vivid experiences for the child and may inspire him to search out books in the library in order to learn more about them. Museum reproductions of such objects frequently mean more to a child than ordinary toys.

Biographies of famous men encountered in school lessons are often some of the favorite reading of bright children. Works suitable for children on the outstanding Presidents, on famous explorers, distinguished scientists, and well-known figures of history are excellent ways to extend a child's interest in what he is learning in school.

Gifted children are often hero worshipers in the best sense of the word. They are impressed by, and interested in, the lives of distinguished people. They enjoy biographies and biographical movies. A group of one hundred gifted boys and girls in the sixth grade chose the following personages as the favorites they liked to read about and gave the characteristics they thought distinguished them. They are listed in order of popularity.

This list is certainly not all-inclusive and does not pretend to rank the "best" people, but it can be used as an identification game and an inspiration to a child to learn about those with whom he is not acquainted.

Amelia Earhart	Brave, fearless
John J. Audubon	Kind, studious, patient
Albert Schweitzer	Brilliant, kind, sage-like
Richard Byrd	Fearless, brave, daring
Walt Disney	Imaginative, resourceful
Marco Polo	Adventurous, determined
Simón Bolívar	Courageous, leader, liberator
O. Henry	Humorous, delightful
Will Rogers	Humorous, observing
Miguel Hidalgo y Castilla	Brave, patriotic, daring
Pablo Picasso	Artistic, modern, creative

Charles Steinmetz	Inventive, persevering
Pëtr Ilich Tchaikovsky	Musical, inventive
Queen Hatshepsut	Historical, interesting, powerful
Hans Christian Andersen	Imaginative, creative
Marie Curie	Ingenious, curious
Thomas Alva Edison	Undaunted, inventive
Mark Twain	Humorous, dramatic
Franz Liszt	Musical, wonderful
Paul Cézanne	Artistic, creative, discerning
Louisa May Alcott	Patient, truthful
Tomás Masaryk	Brave, patriotic
Francisco Goya	Creative, truthful
Edward MacDowell	Talented, beauty-loving
Jahangir	Emperor, designer
J. Edgar Hoover	Intelligent, discerning
Michael Pupin	Inventive, persevering

A child should have basic books of his own, but it is rarely possible to buy him all the volumes he wants or should have. No matter how many books he may have, an introduction to the public library and a card of the child's own should be given high priority.

Many a gifted child whose rapid reading required frequent returns to the library has worked out a special arrangement with a sympathetic librarian that enabled him to borrow more books than is usual. Such children sometimes exhaust the resources of the children's section and gain permission to go on to more adult works. When this cannot be done, a parent or other adult can accompany the child and borrow wanted books for him.

As the child's taste in reading advances, parents often grow concerned that he may read books unsuitable for his years.

Parents with this worry should keep in mind that children who are otherwise clean-minded will not be "corrupted" by incidents described between book covers. In any case, such material cannot be kept from children if they are interested in getting their hands on it. Smut is available for a quarter at almost every newsstand. It is better to let children read adult books freely in the living room than cause them to sneak peeks at forbidden trash away from home.

Actually, children almost always skip over that which is beyond their years. They read novels for plot and action rather than for psychological analysis or specific incidents. One eleven-year-old girl read quickly through *The Scarlet Letter* and reported that she enjoyed it. At the end of the book she still had no idea what The Letter stood for. A twelve-year-old who read *Of Human Bondage* stated that the book interested him but he expressed impatience with the passion-tortured hero.

Parents seeking guidance on what books to acquire for their children often ask for book lists. At Hunter there are none. The purpose of providing a child with books is not to get him through a list of "best books." He needs the books that are best for him, in terms of his individual interests and preferences at a particular time. The child should be guided in his choice of reading but should be allowed to choose by himself most of the books he reads.

The usual consequence of forced reading is a revolt against reading or, at least, a refusal to read the book that is being prescribed. Parents will be more effective in encouraging reading if they let a child's interests serve as the guide. The parent can then suggest or make available worth-while books in that field. If the parent feels he, himself, needs guidance, the teacher or librarian can suggest suitable titles. If the child takes to a suggested book, fine. If not, let the book be put aside for a later time when the youngster may be ready for it.

Children have good literary instincts. Without being able

to explain why, they will usually prefer good books if they are available.

At the same time, they may happily consume a certain number of comic books and other examples of illiterature. So long as these do not displace worth-while books, parents should allow a modest ration of such reading rather than try to ban them completely.

With the current emphasis on the development of scientists, some parents have wondered how forcefully they should attempt to promote their child's interest in science. A child should have an opportunity to explore science in the same manner as he is introduced to art, literature, and other fields. Whether he becomes a scientist or not, he should certainly become acquainted with this area of knowledge, just to be well-informed. Probably the best thing conscientious parents can do is see to it that their child has opportunities at an early age to develop and explore interests in science.

Professor Lewis Terman, the distinguished psychologist who conducted the best-known extensive experiment on the characteristics of the gifted, has stated that scientific aptitude is often shown at a comparatively early age. Professor Edward Teller, the physicist who played the most important role in developing the hydrogen bomb, has advocated exposing children to scientific materials while they are still in elementary school.

This does not mean that only children who show special interest in science while still in elementary school can hope to become scientists. Many of this country's outstanding scientists got interested in their fields in high school and college. Some did not decide on their scientific specialty until they got to graduate school.

Early exposure to scientific materials, however, gives the child with aptitude in this direction the opportunity to explore his interest at an early age. Many children who are given the chance will become interested in science quite

144 WORKING WITH THE GIFTED CHILD

early even if they do not decide to make science their life's work. However, deliberate effort to push a child into science as a vocational goal is no more desirable than pushing him into any other specific field or profession.

With the coverage now being given to science on television, in newspapers, and in magazines, a child will have many added opportunities to read about scientific matters. Biographies of famous scientists, books on science suitable for youngsters, science toys such as chemistry sets, simple microscopes, and similar playthings all give a child the chance to explore his scientific bent. There is no best way to interest a child in science or any other field.

One of the country's experts on electronic computers became interested in science when he received a construction toy at the age of eight. An outstanding physicist, on the other hand, got interested in his field after reading science fiction. Other children have had similar toys and done similar reading and eventually turned to entirely non-scientific fields. Since it is still not known just what makes a person choose a specific vocation, the best recommendation regarding opportunities in science and every other field is: provide the chance but don't force the choice.

Even though they are almost always a good deal older before they finally settle on a vocation, children usually like to think about what they will become when they grow up. Most of the choices are fanciful, of course, with preferences leaning heavily toward adventurous and presumably "glamorous" pursuits.

But it is worth while to encourage a child to think about the qualities different vocations require. It helps him explore what he wants to be like and what he hopes to do. Gifted children asked to list their possible vocational choices and the qualities each would require have produced answers that have unwittingly been both humorous and perceptive. One girl listed the following occupations and the traits required:

"Teacher   — patience
Mother   — understanding
Old Maid   — cheerfulness."

A boy who thought he might like to be a doctor wrote: "I'd need both patience and patients."

The different ways in which equally gifted children can respond to the same opportunity to explore a new field is illustrated by an incident that occurred when a ten-year-old tried to interest his classmates in his special hobby—biology. He persuaded a college student to dissect a frog for the class and induced his teacher to consent to the demonstration.

The teacher cautiously explained in advance what would be done. She invited any child to leave the room who did not feel up to viewing the experiment. Only two left.

Shortly after the demonstration began, a member of the class appeared in the principal's office. Speaking very calmly, and apparently quite undisturbed himself, he reported, "The teacher says, come down, it's an emergency."

"What happened?"

Carefully choosing his words he reported the consequences of the frog experiment up to the moment he had been sent for help. "Three children are green, two are a whitish-yellow, one threw up, and one is flat on the floor. I think he fainted. The teacher was holding one girl's head when I left and I heard the college girl say, 'I'm getting out of here!'"

Attraction to a specific field is not only a question of opportunity, but of individual characteristics. Early exposure to science does, however, give the child with aptitude in this direction a chance to reveal it sooner. The same holds true for every field. If more children get a chance to explore different fields, more of them will undoubtedly reveal aptitudes and skills that might otherwise not have been discovered.

Gifted children frequently explore new interests by making up scrapbooks or assembling materials in file folders and making up their own filing systems. This activity often starts at a simple level in the preschool years and continues in a more advanced manner as the child grows older and his interests get more complex.

While the young child is primarily interested in pictures, the older child is increasingly interested in diagrams, charts, maps, and text. One of the best sources of inexpensive booklets on such diverse subjects as past and present problems in American government, hobbies, how-to activities—such as gardening, photography and other subjects—is the United States Government itself. One way to start is by writing to the Government Printing Office in Washington, D. C., for catalogs of what is available. Other sources of material are State Chambers of Commerce and large corporations. Many of these organizations' advertisements contain offers of printed material that can be secured by writing for them. Several paper-bound books have been published that list hundreds of free and inexpensive booklets and other materials that are available from organizations all over the country.

To parents, the scrapbooks and files put together from all of these materials may look messy and unorganized, but usually the child has a plan. He will include maps, pictures, newspaper clippings, and other materials dealing with the subject in which he is currently interested. More often than is realized, the gifted child will collect data on political, social, and economic problems and prove a shrewder analyst and critic than adults expect.

Stamp and coin collections are popular with school-age children. Collecting stamps can be made more than the accumulation of bits of paper by encouraging a child to learn where different countries are (most youthful stamp collectors were acquainted with Monaco long before a highly publicized wedding), what the people and objects pictured on the stamps represent, and, in general, what the background is of the countries whose stamps they are collecting.

At different times, the gifted child will probably have a variety of collections. He may get interested in rocks, butter-flies, shells, pressed flowers, leaves. Parents should expect, however, that a child's interest may shift fairly quickly when he is young, and not be upset if collections are abandoned just when they seem to be well started. Eventually the child may again get interested in a collection and return to it on a more mature level.

Dropping one interest and picking up another is part of the growing-up process. As the gifted child's mind grows and expands, he becomes aware of new subjects to explore. In his impatience to learn, he may drop what he is doing and start the new interest. In other cases, the child may progress upward through different levels of a single subject. For example, the child who once had fairy tales read to him may progress to an interest in mythology and eagerly read the classic tales of ancient gods and goddesses.

Sometimes one interest leads to another. Children's records, for example, can be followed by folk songs. This attractive music may then inspire the child to try making music himself. Many write new words for old tunes.

Children are often attracted to their family's activities and hobbies. If other members of the family play or sing, the child is more likely to do so. The boy whose father works with tools or likes to fish is likely to want to imitate him. Fishing can lead to nature study and knowledge of the outdoors. The father who does not feel his boy is ready to work in his home workshop can still give the child a few simple tools of his own and let him putter. Children love to tinker with old clocks and radios, even though they usually succeed only in taking them apart.

Model building is another activity that often attracts children and gives them an opportunity to explore their mechanical aptitude. Hand puppets are a good early project for the youthful mechanic. A group of children often make puppets, then design the sets and costumes, and put on their own puppet plays.

A child not only needs materials but also some work and storage space he can call his own. If he has his own bookshelf, file drawer, bulletin board, closet shelf, he has a place to store his materials and books. This encourages him to keep his things in order and makes it easier for mother to enforce rules of tidiness, and he is more likely to keep his things out of places where they are not wanted. By doing a little of his own housekeeping he also learns to appreciate the efforts made in the rest of his home.

One household item that almost every child appropriates as virtually his own is the family television set. While gifted children like to watch television programs as much as other children, they view them more critically than average youngsters. One girl commented on the Westerns: "It is the same story over and over. About the only difference between the shows is the color of the horses."

Like all children, the gifted enjoy the adventure stories and the cartoons. They are also interested, however, in the educational programs. The best way to make sure a child does not spend too much time in front of the television set is to encourage his development of varied interests. Sometimes, a television program, itself, does this. A child may view something that will inspire him to look further into a subject if he has been taught and encouraged to do so.

One girl, writing a class report on a television play she had seen, noted that, "It showed the problems and actions of a teen-ager. She was sent to a school for disturbed children. After watching this play I became interested in psychology. This interest grew bigger with the help of a book about psychology."

One way to lessen the influence of the television set is to give children something else to view that they will find more interesting. Home-movie projectors have become popular and many instructive films can now be purchased or rented. A family can put on its own movie programs of travel films and other worth-while subjects.

Slide projectors and slide viewers can be used the same way. Many color slides of scenes in this country and abroad can be purchased. If father is a camera fan, he and his child can go on picture-taking expeditions together, with the child's interests helping determine what pictures are taken.

One father used to play "newspaper" with his boy. They would go out as a "photographer-reporter" team with father taking pictures based on his youngster's interest at the moment—animals, trains, buildings, etc. When the pictures were developed, the child would project them and report on what he had seen. As he grew older, his trips were treated as assignments and he would write brief news stories describing what he had seen. Another child kept a little diary of the day's events and before bedtime described what she had done that day to her father.

Many communities offer facilities for children with special talents. The local museum or "Y," for example, probably sponsors art classes. Music and dance classes are often similarly available.

As always, parents should keep in mind that they are not to push a child but should guide him. In order to make a child want to learn, he needs to feel he has a say in choosing the direction in which he is going.

Independence is something the gifted crave, and parents should try to give a child as much freedom and initiative as his maturity, rather than his age, allows. One eleven-year-old boy, very large for his age, was called to the office when it was learned the other children were secretly laughing at him. He was asked if he did not think he could forego the carton of milk his mother brought with her at dismissal time. The youngster looked distressed.

"I knew this would happen," he said, "but I hated to hurt her feelings by telling her not to bring it. She still thinks I am her baby, and won't grow without that milk. But I guess it's time for her to stop."

Long after it has become unnecessary, many parents still escort their children to school, pull on their rubbers for them, and perform a variety of personal chores the youngster would prefer—and should prefer—to do for himself. If a child shows above-average maturity for his age, he is entitled to more freedom than other children—as long as he can live up to the responsibility.

CHAPTER TEN

Adolescence: Years of Decision

GIFTED CHILDREN are as susceptible to the strains and pains of adolescence as average young people. They go through the same physical changes, emotional tensions, and social problems, and often at an earlier age. Some gifted children of eleven may exhibit all of the signs of adolescence usually associated with teen-agers.

Facing new distractions and new demands for his time, the gifted adolescent's values may waver. His motivation to study may weaken and his ambition to achieve may lessen. At this point, the gifted child who gets no deep feeling of accomplishment from being successful in his studies, who has not learned to apply himself, and who, therefore, has not acquired self-discipline, will lose interest in intellectual activities. For a child who does not foresee any use for his studies, there will be little attraction in studying when there are so many other activities tempting him.

Parents must now build on the training the gifted child received all through childhood. The adolescent who has learned to value knowledge, and who has been taught that success in school is important to his future, is likely to hold on to these beliefs despite the distractions of the adolescent years. The child who has been coasting through school on

151

his natural abilities, without learning how to concentrate and without being shown the importance of scholastic achievement, often begins to slide downhill in his school work.

Motivation to learn and desire to achieve are developed in gradual stages. They cannot suddenly be drilled into a child when he reaches adolescence. Sometimes, of course, a gifted adolescent who has been drifting along does catch fire when his interests are aroused by a new school subject or when an especially talented teacher inspires him. Suddenly he becomes motivated to learn.

Such a transformation is comparatively rare. A flame can be fanned only where there are sparks. And the adolescent who has not learned to study, whose reading habits are poor, whose interests are limited, is not likely to become suddenly inflamed with a desire for knowledge.

If, however, parents have laid the groundwork during the preadolescent years, the normal distractions and problems of adolescence can be kept under control. When their adolescent was still a child, parents had to be aware of both the special needs created by his giftedness and the normal needs of childhood. In handling the adolescent, parents have the same dual problem. While their teen-ager has the same problems as any other child of this age, his giftedness is an additional factor that must be kept in mind.

Just as they would with any adolescent, parents must determine how much freedom they will allow their gifted teen-ager. The use of the family car, size of allowance, frequency of dates, hours to be observed, are "normal" parent-adolescent problems. They are discussed in many publications. Parents will make their decisions and impose standards based on their reading, discussion, training, and what other parents in their area are doing. The special concern of this chapter, however, is how parents should handle giftedness during adolescence.

Adolescence is the age of conformity. The interests of his age group often determine the adolescent's values. If friends think it is clever to be smart-alecky about school, that scholars are squares, and that life is made for kicks, the gifted adolescent may choose popularity over prudence. He may conceal his ability and purposely do poorly in school. Teen-age girls, particularly, will often conceal their abilities because they are afraid boys will shun them if they appear too bright.

The new wave of interest in the gifted, in science training, and in intellectual achievement is helping to weaken this viewpoint. As the mother of a brilliant teen-age daughter commented, "Lucky for her there's a new trend now. Boys don't mind girls being bright." Parents whose gifted child seems more bent on hiding his gifts than developing them will have to depend on the influence they have built up through the childhood years when they point out the inevitable consequence of such behavior.

Fortunately, the adolescent who has enjoyed intellectual interests in the past is not likely to abandon them—unless he is revolting against parental pressure. Parents who have allowed their child a reasonable measure of freedom and independent choice in the past will find it easier to grant the adolescent increased freedom as he grows more capable of caring for himself. The less the teen-ager has to rebel against, the better chance he will keep concentrating on his self-development.

A gifted adolescent may do poorly in high school for the following reasons:

1. He is not used to applying himself to intellectual activities and therefore does not know how to study.

2. He has not had to concentrate before, is overconfident, and, therefore, fails because he does not make enough effort.

3. He is not interested in school, and, therefore, gives most of his time to outside interests.

4. He is rebelling against his parents and teachers, and shows his "independence" by doing poorly.

5. He sees no value in doing well in school because he has a low vocational goal or no aspirations toward higher education.

Because of these factors, a substantial proportion of gifted adolescents do not go on to college. Studies have shown that lack of motivation is even more important than lack of funds as a reason why high-school graduates with high ability fail to continue their education in college.

If a gifted teen-ager has become convinced, however, of the importance of his schooling, he will have a stabilizer during the years when new interests compete for his time. Tempted by broadened social activities, the opposite sex, and the glamor of increased freedom, he will keep in mind that he must do well enough in school so that his educational plans are not affected. If he has a high vocational goal, even if it is not definite, this will also strengthen his resolve to forge ahead. Together, these influences will keep him from abandoning the rigors of study for more immediate pleasures.

How an adolescent will develop his giftedness during the crucial teen-age years often depends, therefore, on a choice he makes at the time he enters high school. At this point the gifted child has reached a new plateau in his intellectual development. Now, often without realizing the significance of what he is doing, he makes decisions that will affect his entire future.

The adolescent decides what high school to attend. If there is only one school available to him, he still selects the course of studies he will follow. Serious questions about his career are now being answered.

Will he go to college? If he wants to go to college, he has to select an academic course. Will he go to work right after graduating from high school? Then the adolescent may select a vocational or commercial course. Does he just want to get through school without too much effort? Then, if they are available, he may select "snap" courses.

Now, in his early teens, the adolescent is making choices that will determine the opportunities open to him when he graduates from high school. The course he picks now may limit the educational and employment opportunities open to him four years from now.

For example, he may elect a course of study that does not give him the necessary credits for admission to college. Four years later he changes his mind and wants to go on to higher education. At that time, it may be too late. Lacking the required credits, he probably will not be admitted to a college. If he does get admitted, it will probably be on condition that he make up the missing courses. If sufficiently determined, he may then retrace his steps and catch up. More likely, the obstacles will discourage him and he will abandon the idea of higher education.

Even if the adolescent has the determination to correct his mistake he will still have to pay a high price for his earlier decision. He will use up time that he might have employed in further progress. His educational deficiencies will probably keep him from being admitted to the school he would have preferred. He will have lost the intellectual training and discipline he would have acquired through a more rigorous course of study. He will find it more difficult to handle his college studies.

Throughout the country many gifted adolescents are making such mistakes. Not realizing the consequences, they fail to select the high school program that gives them the best opportunity to use their gifts when they graduate from high school.

Today, if one does not get a college education he is automatically eliminated from a great many occupations. Without a college degree it is virtually impossible to become a doctor, lawyer, accountant, engineer, scientist, or a member of almost any of the professions. The day when a bright young man could read law, for example, while serving as a lawyer's clerk is past.

All of the professions now require a college degree and, in addition, usually further training in graduate school after college. Scientists and engineers require long years of academic training before they are considered qualified in their fields. The day of the self-trained inventor who worked in his home-made laboratory is over.

The business world has also changed. From office boy to president of the company is a success story of the past—unless the office boy is a college man working part time or during the summer. Corporations now usually choose their trainees and future executives from the ranks of college graduates. Those without a degree are not often considered for the jobs that can eventually lead to the top.

The intellectually gifted adolescent has the ability to do college work successfully. With a college education, he will have the preliminary training to secure a job that offers him the opportunity to use his abilities to best advantage. No matter how gifted he may be, a young person will almost never be considered for such employment unless he has some college education. He will not be admitted to college unless his high school record is suitable. To make such a record, he must select the proper course. And the decision on the high school course he will take is usually made in his early teens.

What influences an adolescent in deciding what high school program he will select? Probably the most important single influence is his desire to continue to learn.

The gifted adolescent has been developing his motivation to learn and his interest in intellectual achievement all through childhood. On the threshold of his teens, he reaches a new stage in the development of his motivation. Up to now, the gifted child has rarely thought ahead. Desire to learn was based on enjoyment of school, outside interests and hobbies, the desire to please one's parents.

A new and vitally important consideration now influences the gifted adolescent's attitude toward learning. If he expects to go on to college, he knows he must select the course that will prepare him for college. If he already knows he is interested in a vocation that requires higher education and advanced training the decision is easier to make.

Most gifted adolescents starting high school will not yet have decided on a definite vocation. But so long as they know they want to do the kind of work that requires college training they will select the high school program that prepares them for college.

The adolescent's motivation to learn in high school usually depends, therefore, on a vital practical consideration: the kind of future he foresees for himself. If he views a college education as a vital part of his future plans, he will prepare himself properly in high school. If he plans to go to work after finishing high school, or just does not think about the problem at all, he will be much less interested in maintaining a record of academic achievement.

Even if the gifted adolescent definitely decides against a college education, a good high school record is still important. Most of the desirable non-professional jobs that are available today require additional post-high school training. Scientific technicians of all kinds need advanced training. So do the highly skilled workers who fill the most important industrial jobs.

This training may be secured in two-year junior colleges, technical institutes, or apprenticeship programs. In any case, those in charge of these institutions look for high school graduates with good records. Possession of a high I.Q. is not enough.

A young person will usually not be accepted for apprenticeship training in industry, for example, unless he can show a high school record that proves he can study and already has acquired a command of the fundamental tools of learning, such as mathematics and reading. The more complicated that industrial processes become, and the more that automation is introduced into factories, the higher the degree of skill that is required to service and maintain these machines. Many of these skills are taught in special training courses for which young men are carefully selected.

Girls, even when they are gifted, often pay little attention to their educational programs because they do not expect to work for more than a few years after they leave school. Studies have revealed, however, that approximately 30% of all married women continue to work even after they have children. They may stay home for a few years while their children are young, but then they go back to work.

Many other women return to work when their children are grown. These women are often still young enough to have many years ahead of them in which to follow work careers.

Obviously, if so many women are going to spend a substantial part of their lives as paid employees they should prepare themselves to qualify for the best jobs they can find. Women are now being hired for more and more jobs that once were closed to them and their opportunities are expanding all the time. According to the U. S. Census Bureau there are at least some women working in every one of the more than four hundred different occupations the Bureau classifies.

The demand for highly trained personnel is expected to grow continually. To take advantage of these opportunities, young women will need the education and training that qualifies them for such jobs. Here again, a good high school record is the crucial prerequisite for self-advancement.

In order to get gifted teen-agers to make the best use of their gifts, parents should concentrate on inducing them to select the high school program that will enable them to continue their education after the graduate. If the adolescent already has a vocational goal that requires advanced education the task is easier.

Most adolescents do not have a definite vocational goal, however, and it is not necessary for a teen-ager to have picked his occupation in order to convince him that education is important. So long as his aspirations are in the direction of jobs that require advanced education, he will be motivated to do well in high school.

The parents' task, therefore, is to build up the adolescent's ambition so that it is on a level with his gifts. The best time to start, of course, is before the crisis is reached. Fathers are an important influence, since children are always interested in the work their fathers do. The child may not want to hold the same job as father does, and his father may not want him to, but he learns about a whole field of work, the opportunities in it, and the preparation required.

Even if they have not gone to college themselves, or if the fathers holds a comparatively modest position that did not require much academic preparation, parents can imbue a child with the desire for advanced training by the attitudes they express. If education is spoken of with high regard, if the child is impressed with the value of advanced training, if intellectual interests in general are made an important part of family living, the child will be developing the motivation and ambition that will induce him to continue studying hard in high school.

Studies have shown that most high school graduates have attitudes toward further education similar to those of their parents. In homes where education is highly regarded by the parents, the children are usually interested in continuing their own training. Most of the capable high school graduates who fail to continue their education come from homes where education gets little attention.

At the same time that they are encouraging a child, parents should resist the temptation to dictate his choice of a vocation. Many children have been pushed into the same field as their fathers or into a field that one of the parents had originally hoped to enter himself. More than one parent has relieved his own frustration by inducing a child to go into the work the parent had dreamed of doing. Even more common is parental pressure for the child to enter the family business.

If a child becomes genuinely interested in a field the parent suggests, or in continuing to develop the business interests of his father, there is certainly nothing wrong with this. But a child should be allowed to decide for himself and it should be expected he will change his mind more than once before he comes to a final decision.

The child's eventual choice of a vocation should be based as much as possible on genuine preference and interest rather than on pressures exerted from outside or choices based on current reports about particular shortages of personnel. It is not particularly wise to select or reject a field of work because there are too many or too few people in it at the moment.

Probably the best example of such a mistake was the statement made shortly before the Korean War that engineers were so plentiful the country would be oversupplied with them for years to come. The picture changed shortly afterward and the call for scientists and engineers has grown louder every year.

Now the problem is somewhat reversed and there is a certain amount of danger that those who would prefer other fields will be pushed into science and engineering. The country needs highly trained persons in every field and a child should be allowed to follow his personal inclination.

What is most important is that a child should develop interests that are strong enough to lead him eventually to a definite vocational choice. Studies have shown that adults who deliberately selected the work they wanted to do, and then went into such work, are comparatively happy at their jobs. Those who drifted into their occupations, or had their work picked for them, are usually dissatisfied.

Some parents make the error of thinking the gifted adolescent can solve the problem of choosing a career by taking a set of psychological tests. These parents often assume that, since a test once revealed their youngster's I.Q., other tests can now point out where he will find his greatest vocational success.

Actually, if a gifted adolescent has been exploring his interests and abilities since childhood, vocational testing is not likely to tell him much about himself he does not already know. Aptitude and interest tests might reveal, for example, that an adolescent has outstanding mathematical or verbal ability, that he likes dealing with people or prefers working by himself, that he is most interested in science, or mechanics, or art—all facts that the gifted child and his parents are already acquainted with if they have been working together to develop the youngster's gifts. It is highly unlikely that a previously undiscovered ability will be revealed by a test during adolescence.

A person who has paid little attention to the development of his abilities and has done little to explore a variety of interests may receive helpful guidance from vocational tests. But, as one psychologist who has studied aptitude testing and placement for one of the country's largest corporations commented, "If a person has to be told what his interests are, he is not likely to be especially interested in anything."

Contrary to widespread belief, vocational tests do not pinpoint the specific job that the person tested should select. They simply reveal an individual's general aptitudes and preferences. From this a counselor can suggest fields in which one's abilities might be used. There are many occupations into which any one person might fit. The ultimate choice depends on the individual's preference.

If, for example, he shows verbal skill, a high degree of analytical ability, and likes to deal with people, should he become a journalist, a psychologist, a business executive, or a lawyer? The tests will not tell him. His personal interests and preferences will have to guide him and his opportunities will help him decide.

One of the important activities of the teen-ager, therefore, is to learn about various occupations, the education and training they require, and where this preparation can be secured. Unfortunately, many high schools provide little vocational guidance or none at all. According to a study made several years ago, only half the country's high school students had available the advice of a school guidance counselor. Even the schools that have guidance service usually can provide only the minimum of assistance. Many high schools offer a one-day discussion of job opportunities to seniors about to graduate. The student really needs such guidance four years earlier, so he would know how to prepare himself for what he wants to do after being graduated.

If a student is fortunate, his school will be able to give him individual help in exploring his vocational interests or can refer him to an outside agency that can help him. Some schools invite distinguished local citizens to lecture on their work. Most of the time, however, he is on his own.

Gifted students will usually have to conduct their own research programs to learn about vocational requirements and job opportunities. First of all, whatever information is in the school should be used. If there is a guidance counselor, he can tell the student what materials are available. Usually the school library will have a section devoted to books and pamphlets that offer vocational information and guidance.

These publications will also reveal where further information can be had.

The United States Department of Labor in Washington, D. C., publishes vocational guidance material. It can be secured by writing to the Department. The public library may contain such publications and can turn out to be a good source of vocational guidance information.

Personal research is another way the gifted adolescent can learn about vocations. Almost every child first gets an idea of different kinds of work by observing what occupations people hold in his community. The information gathered in this way, however, is usually limited to a few of the professions such as medicine, law, and pharmacy; small business, such as retailing; services, like repairmen; and whatever local industry is in the area.

All teen-agers, and the gifted certainly, need much broader information. If somebody in the community is doing the kind of work the adolescent thinks he may be interested in, he should try to learn about it from him. Visits to local businesses and plants are valuable. In newspapers and magazines, with their descriptions of men's achievements all over the country, he can read about many more of the occupations held in our complex society. As he explores different interests through the books he reads, the gifted adolescent will become aware of still other vocational possibilities.

College catalogs are a valuable source of information and most high schools have a fairly good selection of them. There are also comprehensive guides that outline the facilities and special programs offered by most of the colleges in the country. These catalogs and references are often in the public library.

Through such catalogs the adolescent can learn what courses to take in order to be admitted to different colleges. He can find out also the required college program for preparation in different fields and perhaps prepare himself better by selecting certain courses while still in high school. Advanced high school work in science, mathematics, or languages can often make things easier in college. As the teen-ager reads the descriptions of the wide variety of courses offered in college, he will broaden his understanding of what different fields of study are like, and what preparation they require. This may help him decide what he wants to do.

Part-time jobs and summer jobs are other valuable ways for a teen-ager to become acquainted with different kinds of work. Even though the job opportunities available to a youngster of this age are limited, such work gives him the chance to learn something about standards and requirements of paid employment. Often he will clear up mistaken notions about a particular job's "glamor."

Information about vocational interests will come to the youngster in many indirect ways. A hobby or participation in a school club may spark his interest in a particular field. Every activity that widens an adolescent's adult acquaintanceships and broadens his knowledge of people is particularly valuable at this time. They will help him to increase his understanding of adult work and responsibility. Working on the school paper is often valuable, not necessarily because it introduces him to journalism, but because it will probably permit him to meet more teachers and other adults than he would otherwise. Very often, an inspiring teacher, met through a classroom course or an after-school activity, plays a decisive role in determining a teen-ager's future plans.

Not all of the adolescent's activities should have a specific vocational purpose, of course. Yet the value of all these activities in providing vocational information and strengthening motivation for further education should be kept in mind by parents trying to help the child make the right choice in regard to his schooling. As the adolescent progresses through his teens, much of what he does and learns influences the vocational and educational decisions he is making. So long as parent and child are aware of the importance of these decisions, they will be better able to work together in helping the adolescent decide how to make the best use of his gifts.

CHAPTER ELEVEN

The Most Highly Gifted Children

Psychologist Leta Hollingworth, a pioneer
in the study of giftedness, once pointed out that children
with I.Q.'s of 140 probably waste half their time in the ordinary classroom; children with I.Q.'s of 170, she noted, probably waste almost all of their classroom time.

Professor Hollingworth made a special study of children
with I.Q.'s of 180 and above to learn what they were like and
how their enormous promise might be developed more effectively. Children with this kind of intellectual gift are rare.
Statistically, there are less than a handful in a million children.

One reader of this book may have such a child. This chapter is being written not only for one reader, however, but for
all. The problems of the extremely gifted child are like most
of the problems of the "average" gifted child, only more so.
Because the need for certain kinds of care, attention, and
understanding is even more urgent, it illustrates more forcefully the needs of all gifted children.

Occasionally we read of a child who is entering college in
his early teens. The newspapers describe how he taught
himself to read at an age when most other children can
barely speak sentences, began to study algebra while other

166

children were still befuddled by decimal points, finished high school when most of his age group have barely started, and was in almost every way completely beyond and out of touch with his age group.

Reading such descriptions, even the parents of gifted children might wonder how to cope with the needs of such a child. Knowing the effort required to meet the intellectual needs of an "average" gifted child, they understand the enormous difficulty of raising a child whose intellectual achievement is far beyond even most of the gifted children his age.

When such a child appears, he is frequently expected to be as precocious socially and emotionally as he is intellectually. He often grows bewildered and lonely in a world that usually cannot understand the help he requires. He may fail to live up to the almost impossible expectations held for him. If this happens, the old cliches about genius burning itself out are revived and many people grow more convinced than ever that brilliance is an unhealthy sign in a child.

In one sense it is true that it is "dangerous" to show too much intellectual precocity at a young age. The danger is that the child will not get the help he needs to make the most of his rare gift and as a consequence will suffer rather than benefit. A child whose I.Q. places him in the category of "extremely gifted" needs to be as fortunate as he is gifted. He should be born into a family that understands him, is willing to help him, and can secure for him the facilities he needs to develop his extraordinary ability. As understanding of the gifted increases, and the facilities for their education improve, the chances get better that an extremely gifted child will have this kind of good fortune.

The child with an extremely gifted mind is an intellectual prodigy just as a child with extraordinary talent for playing an instrument is a musical prodigy. Both have similar promise and both must surmount similar hurdles. However, the child with a performing gift is more fortunate in several ways: Once his gift is recognized, it is usually accepted; there are known ways of developing it; on the whole, he is not expected to be equally gifted in other aspects of his development. In fact, allowance is often made for possible deficiencies because so much time is devoted to the development of his gift.

The intellectual prodigy, on the other hand, has no single aspect of his development on which adults can concentrate. They therefore find it more difficult to understand his needs and to help him. Because his mentality is so exceptionally advanced, adults often make the mistake of thinking he will be older than his years in every way.

He thinks and speaks like someone almost twice his age. Therefore they expect him to behave and to feel in the same mature way. Adults may consider him virtually an adult in child's clothes. Actually, he has a child's heart, soul, and body, no matter how advanced his mind. He has the same need of his parents, the same longing for companionship, the same delight in play as other children.

Like the performing prodigy, the intellectual prodigy is subject to all the unfortunate consequences of having his gifts exploited. The youthful musician, for example, is not a finished performer. While he is young he attracts attention, not because he is a mature artist, but because he is so advanced for his years. As he approaches adulthood, the standards by which he is judged change. Before, it was enough to be precocious. Now, he must match the achievement of other adult performers.

The frequent penalty of premature exploitation is that the child who is rushed before the public too soon fails to develop his gifts properly. A talent must be long and carefully nurtured through years of study and training before it is fully developed. If a child is shown off, his training is often neglected. The flaws in his preparation become apparent when he grows older and cannot compete with others who originally showed less promise but have been better prepared.

This holds true whether the extremely gifted child is a musician, artist, or scholar. He can be compared in some ways to an extremely talented high school athlete. He is far better than others of his age, and promises to be an outstanding performer, but he still needs time to develop his full capacities. Expecting a prodigy to perform like an adult is similar to requiring the city's all-star high school halfback to be able to play with professionals.

While these problems have become increasingly understood in regard to musical and artistic prodigies, the intellectual prodigy is comparatively neglected. Often he is heedlessly labelled a "genius" and the public then stands back critically and challenges him to prove himself. Professor Hollingworth has pointed out that a child with an exceptionally high I.Q. may be considered a "potential genius." But until he proves himself by creative and original achievement he cannot be considered more than exceptionally promising.

A distinguished psychiatrist, Ernest Jones, who was a student and biographer of Sigmund Freud, has listed the traits shown by recognized scientific geniuses. This listing summarizes the way an outstanding researcher thinks. The traits Dr. Jones lists are:

1. Love of truth.
2. A way of looking at a problem that gives him a different view of it than others get.
3. A seemingly intuitive understanding of what part of a problem is really important even before the evidence has been collected to prove its importance.
4. Periods of intense effort and hard work, continued despite apparent lack of results, which are then followed by what outsiders consider to be "sudden inspiration."
5. A skeptical attitude toward what others consider to be

facts "proven" beyond question and a willingness to consider entirely new answers to such questions.

6. A capacity for intense and prolonged concentration.

Of all the gifted children who have attended Hunter Elementary School, only a few seemed to show all of these traits at an early age. One who has already gained distinction was a twenty-year-old college senior when he was hailed for working out a mathematical problem that professional mathematicians had not been able to solve.

The extremely gifted mind can work harder and faster than less able minds. It also has a way of leaping ahead and visualizing new possibilities where less capable intellects must plod forward slowly, restricted by more limited vision.

Even an extremely gifted child, however, will not necessarily grow up to be a genius. Another gifted child, although he did not show quite as much promise while young, may turn out to be the kind of enormously original and creative adult who deserves to be called a genius.

There is no sure way of predicting what kind of adult the average gifted child will become. It is just as difficult to make predictions about the extremely gifted. All that experts can say is that the extremely gifted child has an exceptionally good chance of becoming an outstanding adult—if he gets the proper care and attention.

The extremely gifted child needs special attention because his extraordinary abilities put him in danger of becoming completely isolated from other children of his age. By the time he enters school he may know so much more than other children that their school problems leave him bored. His vocabulary and sentence structure is usually so far in advance of his classmates that they may find it difficult to understand him. Placed in a class of average children, who may be almost half his mental age, he often has nothing to do. The teacher is kept busy by the rest of the class and has little time to help him.

He may be labelled "queer" and "stuck up" by resentful, misunderstanding children who cannot keep up with him. If the others make fun of him he may begin to dislike school and turn against learning, or simply withdraw to the isolation of his books and lose the advantages of companionship and play with his age mates.

Usually the extremely gifted child is bewildered when other children reject him. When he first enters school, he rarely considers himself different from other children. Often, in fact, he worries that he may not be bright enough. He uses a comparatively adult vocabulary because his thinking is so much more mature than other children; not, unless he has been spoiled, because he is trying to impress anyone.

The thought processes of an extremely gifted child are illustrated by a seven-year-old who turned out to have an I.Q. of more than 200. Asked by a psychologist what he particularly disliked, he replied: "I dislike fighting and arguments very much. As a rule, they are needless, and quite pointless, since nothing is ever settled by them."

The very first school day of one child with an I.Q. of 185 highlights the problems faced by the extremely gifted child. As the teacher started the first reading lesson, he got bored. As the lesson went on, he got restless, and began twisting in his seat. Finally, he picked himself up and left the room. As a four-year-old, he had read his baby-sitter's high school biology text. Obviously there was nothing for him to do in first grade.

Finding a way to keep the extremely gifted child busy in elementary school is usually the first serious problem that confronts his parents. Before he enters school he teaches himself and he can usually keep busy even if his parents do hardly more than supply him with books and materials. Since he learns with extraordinary rapidity, parents are often so gratified that they help him even if they do not realize the extent of his giftedness.

The extremely gifted child does not necessarily reveal his special degree of giftedness by how early he begins talking or reading. Once he does begin these activities, however, his progress is so rapid that he may soon outstrip his age mates.

The difficulty of judging just how gifted the very young child may be is illustrated by reported differences in the time at which a number of extremely gifted children began speaking and reading. The child with an I.Q. of 185 described before, who was an accomplished reader when he began school, was three years old before he spoke. But he must have been learning to read even before he chose to speak, since he was soon reading newspapers aloud. Another extremely gifted child, who several years ago became at thirteen the third youngest student ever to enter Harvard, was reading the letters of the alphabet before he was two.

During the preschool years the extremely gifted child usually gets along with most of the other children his age. As a rule, he is satisfied to share their games. He is physically about average, or at least not sufficiently better to call attention to himself.

When he gets to school the intellectual difference between himself and his companions is fully revealed. Before, he could pursue his intellectual interests at home. Now, he must often sit idly in school. Every time he opens his mouth to recite he reveals how far ahead of the class he has already advanced.

Without special attention the extremely gifted child will soon exhaust whatever resources the ordinary elementary school can offer him. The problem of educating such a child results from the difficulty of creating for him a school environment that will stimulate his interests and challenge him to learn. The same problem exists for all gifted children; for the extremely gifted, the problem is even more acute.

If an extremely gifted child is kept with other children his age he often completes the work of the grade in a short time and has nothing to do unless he is accelerated to the next grade. Fred Safier, who entered Harvard at thirteen, had advanced to the second grade of elementary school within a few weeks. A month later he completed the second grade and was ready for the third.

Such rapid acceleration creates another problem. An extremely gifted child may be able to go through elementary school so quickly that he soon leaves his contemporaries far behind. But physically, socially, and emotionally such a child is not ready for advanced schooling, even if he can meet the academic requirements.

In the case just described, and in most other instances where schools have handled prodigies successfully, the solution has been to combine acceleration and enrichment. Such a program can be worked out only if the school arranges an individual program for the youngster. Some private schools do this and a few public schools also adjust the curriculum for these exceptional pupils.

An extremely gifted child needs the companionship of other bright children. Even if their abilities do not equal his, they are intelligent enough to appreciate his abilities and share some of his interests. He will, therefore, have classmates who are friendly rather than antagonistic.

For as long as possible the extremely gifted child should be in a class whose members are close enough to his age level for him to make friends with them even if his work is more advanced. In addition, his teachers and parents will have to work with him so that he comes to accept and understand that his superiority makes him different. This difference, however, should not be allowed to make him feel he is "peculiar."

If an extremely gifted child is given the opportunity to learn as much as he is capable, he may reach the point where he finally must make a crucial jump. Having exhausted the resources of the schooling available to him so long as he remains with children of approximately his age, he faces the alternative of either marking time or moving far ahead of his age group.

If he has exhausted all the available opportunities for learning, it may be more desirable to send the child ahead, even if in extreme cases it means he starts college in his early teens. The frustration of the brilliant child who is held back because he must wait for the rest of his class was stated by a famous physicist in describing some of his own school experiences: "It's no fun to turn the pages of a book and say, 'yes, yes, of course, I know that.'"

In such cases it may be better to accelerate the youngster and work out another plan for his social life. Fred Safier, for example, found that his Harvard classmates generally accepted him as an intellectual companion even though most of his play was shared with students at a nearby preparatory school.

Norbert Wiener, an outstanding mathematician famous for his work in the development of electronic brains, was a child prodigy who was in college at an age similar to young Safier. In his autobiography, *Ex-Prodigy*, he has described the problem of being virtually a man intellectually while still a child in almost every other way. He, too, found intellectual companionship among his fellow students and playmates among children of his own age.

Extremely gifted children who do not go through school at such a rapid pace still face the problem of adjusting to their intellects. Like a youth of extraordinary physical strength, who must keep his muscles under careful check until he learns to control their power, the youthful possessor of an extraordinarily strong intellect often finds it a painful task to find a place for himself and his capabilities.

Possession of unusual capacities does not automatically give one an insight into how best to use them. The extremely gifted child must also explore various interests until he finds the field in which he wishes to apply his abilities. Meanwhile, parents should refrain from trying to impose their own choice on the youngster.

It is probably not a coincidence that a mind such as Norbert Wiener's is attracted to physics and mathematics. The kind of abstract reasoning ability such fields require are particularly suited to this kind of intellect. Still, this does not mean that every extremely gifted child will be attracted to such fields as nuclear physics and pure mathematics.

So long as a field offers a sufficient intellectual challenge it will attract the gifted. For example, Adolph A. Berle, who entered Harvard at fourteen, has gained distinction in government and law. He served as assistant Secretary of State, represented this country abroad as an ambassador, and is a leading expert on corporate law.

Child prodigies, despite the difficulties they face, obviously can become well-balanced and productive adults. Other extremely gifted children, while their early school careers may not be quite as unusual as those mentioned, have similarly gone on to distinguished achievement as adults.

The difficulties of adjustment encountered by the extremely gifted child ilustrate many of the problems faced by all those who are gifted. Some parents, wondering how actively to encourage their child in intellectual and artistic pursuits, question whether "it is worth it."

As one troubled mother put it: "Won't he just be unhappy

if he thinks about things too much? Maybe he'll be happier if he's like most people and lets somebody else do the heavy thinking. There's too much to worry about nowadays."

This parent was trying to find the best way to promote her child's future welfare, but she was making a few common and erroneous assumptions. The gifted individual is usually not unhappier than other people. There is a good chance, in fact, that he will be happier than most, just as studies have shown that gifted children are usually better adjusted than other youngsters.

Despite the old saying, ignorance is not bliss. A large number of people are bored a good deal of the time. They spend much of their leisure looking for ways "to kill time." When they are free to do anything they want, they often do not know what they want to do.

The gifted, well-developed mind, on the other hand, is usually an occupied mind. Whether busy with work or play, it usually has enough interests so that it is not bored. Most people are happiest on the infrequent occasions when they are being creative. Creativity is one of the marks of gifted-ness. The gifted, therefore, usually spend more time at activities that make them happy than most other people.

The mother who thought her gifted child might be hap-pier if he "lets somebody else do the heavy thinking," failed to consider that many of the most unhappy people spend a large part of their time fretting about comparative triviali-ties. The extent of one's unhappiness is rarely determined by the significance of one's concerns. A trait of the ignorant is that they usually worry excessively about the compara-tively unimportant. One of the satisfactions of the gifted is that they concern themselves with problems they feel are important and whose solution gives them deep personal pleasure.

There are problems in being gifted that the average are

unlikely to encounter. There are compensations, however, that the average hardly know. No parent can successfully weigh the problems and compensations of being gifted and decide for his child how much of his giftedness it will make him happiest to develop.

A child's gifts are part of his whole being. Parents, having given their child life, and thereby his gifts, must help him make the most of his gifts if they would help him make the most of his life.

Index

Parents—(*Continued*)
  guidance of child, vii-viii, 19,
    32, 58-59, 60, 63, 65-66,
    68, 78, 149
  and Parents' Association, 69, 70,
    72
  position of father, 28, 54, 61-
    62, 64, 72, 77, 92-93, 159
  pressures of, 13, 28, 50, 52-56,
    57, 77, 79, 80-82, 115
  relation to school and teacher,
    vii-viii, 112-115, 119, 135-
    136
Pets, 94
Phonograph records, 105
Physical development, 7, 16, 76,
    77, 113, 116-117
Popularity, 69, 153
Praise, 51, 67, 104
Precocity, 30, 167
Preschool period, 12-14, 62, 85-
    109
Prodigies, 30, 167-175
Protectiveness, parental, 48-49,
    56-57, 150
Punishment, in discipline, 126

Questions, child's, 12, 15, 62-63,
    65, 137-138
Quiz Kids, 54, 55, 64

Reading:
  choice of books, 98, 139-140,
    142
  readiness for, 14, 90-92, 172
  reference books, 63, 64, 137
  undesirable material, 141-142,
    143
Reasoning skill, 25, 125
Recreation, 8, 59
Religious interest, 15-16, 113
Reports, school's to parents, 50,
    122

Responsibility, 150
Rewards, 115
Rhymes and rhyming, 98-99

Schools:
  acceleration of child in, 116-
    118, 173
  enrichment of programs in, 114,
    116, 118-119
  gifted child in:
    college, 17, 75, 134, 154-157
    high school, 75, 134, 153-
      155, 156
    kindergarten, 90
    nursery school, 87-90
  special classes for gifted child,
    57, 59, 110, 118, 135
Schoolwork, and child, 22, 41,
    111, 112-113, 114
Science, 26, 103, 143-144, 145
Self-control, 124
Siblings, 121-123
Skipping, in school, 116
Social development, 51, 53, 76-
    77, 108, 113, 117
Spatial skill, 24-25
Sports, 40, 59, 77, 108
Storytelling, child's, 132-133

Talented child, definition of, 29
Talking, early, 13, 172
Teachers, and the gifted child, 18,
    22, 41, 59, 111, 113, 122,
    136-137, 164
Television, 91, 148-149
Terman, Lewis, 16-18, 75, 143
Toys, 93-94
Trips, 72, 106-107

Unpopularity, 69, 131-132, 170-
    171

Verbal skill, 13-14, 23-24